The Millennial's Guide to Wealth

Learn About Saving, Investing, Spending and Living While Drinking Beer

Barry Pencek

Copyright © 2016 Barry Pencek
All rights reserved.
Printed in the United States of America

ISBN-10: 154115455X
ISBN-13: 978-1541154551

"One of the main things Barry teaches in this book is to never stop learning. That's my number one philosophy. In clear language, with ideas you can act on immediately, Barry helps you build a solid present and an exciting financial future. My favorite advice of all, though, is to remember to listen more than you talk, because that's how you learn."

Clark Howard, nationally syndicated consumer guru

Dedication

To my boys, for without them I would have had no compulsion to even begin, let alone finish such a book.

Acknowledgments

This book would never have been completed were it not for the advice, support and encouragement from a lot of people. The first thing I did when I seriously decided to finish this project was to call a couple writers I knew to get some guidance on how to proceed. Warren Thompson and John "Tilt" Meyer pointed me in the right direction and opened my eyes to what was ahead after I got the words down on paper.

Faith Meyer Yeung, my copy editor, gets my undying gratitude for her patience as I made numerous changes to the manuscript. She further enlightened me about the publishing process.

It's said a picture's worth a thousand words, so I must acknowledge Larry McQuaid and B.J Ralston of DST Retirement Solutions of New York for the use of the investing chart from Wealth Management Systems. B.J. in particular, graciously helped me get through a snafu of my own making regarding a licensing agreement, for which I am grateful. Likewise, permission to use the chart created by Dr. Marc Faber is greatly appreciated and saved another thousand words.

I also want to thank Dr. Richard H. Rahe, MD, for giving permission to use his *Social Readjustment Rating Scale*.

After striking out with numerous educational institutions, Chris Summers of the Financial Aid Office at Oglethorpe University helped make the murky waters of student loans just a little bit clearer.

I must thank Josh Langston, teacher, editor, cover designer, sounding-board, and friend. He took my Open Office scrawl from an old Windows Vista computer and gave it form. If it weren't for his thoughtful and insightful guidance I never would have finished this endeavor.

And finally to my true love and partner in life, my wife Mary who has endured my craziness the last few years. Whether waking in the middle of the night to get some thoughts in my head on paper or abandoning her to do research, she never complained. She has provided support and encouragement as this book went from idea, to project, to obsession, to completion. Thanks luv.

Contents

Introduction	xi
I. Saving	**2**
The Big Picture	3
The Risk Shift	4
ERISA	6
IRAs	8
Mom, Apple Pie, Baseball and Debt	10
South Dakota Saves Citibank	12
Know Thyself	14
Spendthrifts & Frugalers	16
Uncle Dick and Uncle Trev	19
Pay Yourself First	22
Write It Down	23
The Emergency Fund	26
The Retirement Fund	26
Other Challenges	28
The Miracle of Compounding	29
A Double Edged Sword	30
The Bottom Line	32
II. Investing	**33**
The Big Picture	35
Creative Destruction	36
Moola	39
Stocks	40
Bonds	42
Time Horizon	46
Trading vs. Investing	47
Market Timing	48
A Couple of Smart Guys	49
We're Only Human	52
Mow The Grass	55
Selecting a Partner	56
Risk Tolerance	60
Fraudsters About	61
Mutual Funds	61
The World is Your Oyster	66
Morningstar	67
Exchange Traded Funds	67
Building Your Portfolio	68
Option One - Target Funds	69
Option Two - Index Funds	71
Option Three - Managed Funds	72
Option Four - Individual Stocks	73
Dollar Cost Averaging	74
The Taxman Cometh	75
Other Forms of Investing	77
Mega-Trends	80
The Bottom Line	83
III. Spending	**85**
The Big Picture	87
Windfalls	87
Debt	90
Not All Debt is Created Equal	93
The 800 Pound Gorilla	95
Investing in Yourself	97
STEM	98
529	105
Wheels	106
The Budget	108
Paper or Plastic	109
Never Pay Retail	111
Never Borrow For Lifestyle	113
The Talk	115

DC-5	115
Credit Reports	117
Credit Scores	119
Insurance	120
Retirement	123
I Want It, And I Want It Now!	126
The Big Warm Fuzzy	127
The Bottom Line	128

IV. Living   **129**

The Big Picture	131
What is Wealth?	131
Can Money Buy Happiness?	132
Virtues	133
Don't Be a Waste of Skin	136
Giving	137
Leadership	139
Don't Judge a Book By Its Cover	141
Health	143
Move	146
Eat	148
Chill	153
Head Games	156
Helicopters	157
Assume You've Been Hacked	158
Zombie Apocalypse	161
Friends	162
Learn to Listen	163
Homework	164
The Bottom Line	165

Epilogue   167

The Intergalactic Web	169
Would You Like Fries With That?	171
Thank You	173

For My Sons   **177**

About the Author   **180**

Introduction

To a certain extent this is a book about generations. Originally I wanted to pass on to my sons Rod, Sam, James and Andrew, some of the financial and other lessons I've learned as I've gone through life. With perfect 20/20 hindsight, I realize I've made some stupid and asinine mistakes, not unlike many have made before me and others will make in the future. Unlike other species, we humans are supposed to build upon what previous generations have learned to keep from "reinventing the wheel," but unfortunately it doesn't always work that way, especially when it comes to saving, investing and spending money.

Shortly after retiring from a career in aviation in 2006, I started volunteering at consumer advocate Clark Howard's Consumer Action Center, answering calls from people around the country. I soon discovered it's not just my boys who need to improve their financial literacy. Today's Millennial generation, and even Generation X before them, are making the same mistakes I made when I was their age. It can partially be blamed on human nature, but is mostly a frightening lack of financial knowledge at a time when it's more important than ever to have at least a basic understanding of financial matters. So, this book has sections on saving, investing, and spending money, plus a fourth section about living, which is why it's a guide to "Wealth," and not just a guide to "Money."

It takes four things to accumulate monetary wealth: some basic knowledge, a little seed money, time, and self-discipline, with self-discipline by far being the most difficult. But first you have to know what type of person you are so you can capitalize on your strengths and mitigate your weaknesses, because human nature plays a big role in everything we do, not only regarding money. Knowing yourself is the most important key to success. If you don't understand who you are, you can become your own worst enemy and later in life, in one of those would've-should've-could've moments, look back and realize that you, too, made a lot of stupid, asinine mistakes. Hopefully, through this book, my boys and anyone else who reads it, can avoid many of the more common ones.

Trust me when I say what's presented here is not rocket science, and there are no groundbreaking theories or formulas unveiled. Saving, investing and spending can be as simple or as complex as you'd like to make it. There are however, some common sense and logical things that everyone should know, and once they're understood, the road to success will be much easier. Since most of the book is about money a good bit of time is devoted to the "why" of saving, investing and spending because I believe if you understand why you should do something, you're more likely to do it. We'll also touch on the psychology behind our human behavior when it comes to making decisions.

I wrestled quite a bit with the title and changed it several times. Originally it was to be ***How To Accumulate Wealth: A Father's Financial and Other Advice to His Sons***. As it morphed into advice for young people in general, I decided it would be better to give it a title with a more defined focus and thought about ***A Young Person's Guide to Wealth (too boring),* or even *The Generation X, Y and Z Guide to Wealth*** (too confusing). I finally settled on ***The Millennial's Guide to Wealth…*** (even though Rod and his wife, Rae, are Generation X'ers, and their children, Christian, Jack and Dylan, are Generation Z), because the Millennials are the new 800 pound gorilla in the demographic room, and as we'll see, are certainly in need of guidance.

The subtitle switched to beer because I like beer; my boys like beer, and just about every Millennial I know likes beer, so I thought beer might lighten the mood and entice more

Millennials to pick the book up and peruse it. All that said, I believe anyone of any age with a desire to improve themselves and their financial literacy, whether or not they drink beer, would benefit from reading it.

One problem with writing a book for Millennials is that they range in age from high school students to thirty-somethings, married with children. Talk about diverging interests! Realizing that a book can't be all things to all people, it is skewed toward Millennials in their mid-twenties and older because the teenager will soon be a twenty-something or even thirty-something (gasp!)

But if you're now in your thirties, I'm sorry to inform you that you can't go back to your high school days. That ship has sailed. If you happen to be a teenager reading this, I ask that you not throw it away when, or if, you finish it. Just set it aside for now and dig it out on your twenty-something birthday, or when Jason Bourne comes out of hiding for the eleventh time, and reread it. It'll make more sense then.

It seems that Millennials, like every other generation in their youth, have an aversion to personal finance. Admittedly, it can be a very dull, if not downright painful subject, and some would rather watch paint dry than buy, let alone read such a book. But these are exactly the people who need it the most. In an effort to make the subject a little more palatable, throughout the pages you'll find numerous sidebars, some with amplifying information, others with humorous subject related trivia, and a few with totally unrelated but hopefully interesting factoids.

One final thing: the dreaded disclaimer. I don't have CPA, CFP, CFA, ChFC, or any other letters after my name. My entire professional career has been as a pilot, flying in the Marine Corps or with commercial airlines. Although I have been investing for more than forty years, I am not an investment professional, and all the financial advice in this book, though based on common sense, is strictly one layman's opinion and should be taken as such.

Thanks.

Barry

Generations

While there are no official names and definitions for particular generations of Americans, society does tend to lump them into various groups. The dates sometimes overlap depending on who is writing about them. Here's a thumbnail sketch.

The Lost Generation (born 1890 to 1900) The term was initially used in Great Britain when referring to those who died in WWI but was later popularized in American literature as those who "lost" their pre-war values in the fast changing post-war era.

The Interbellum Generation (born 1901 to 1913) Meaning "between the wars." They were too young to have been in WWI and too old to be in WWII. They came of age in the Roaring Twenties and the Great Depression.

The GI Generation (born 1910 to 1925) Came of age during the Roaring Twenties, the Great Depression and WWII. In 1998, newsman Tom Brokaw wrote *The Greatest Generation*, detailing their wartime service, and that new handle seems to have stuck.

The Silent Generation (born 1926 to 1945) Small in numbers, these children of the Lost and Interbellum Generations, mostly grew up in the hardscrabble times of the Great Depression and the Dust Bowl. The name comes from a 1951 *Time* Magazine article in which they were described as being quiet, cautious, hard workers who conformed to society. They were savers.

Baby Boomers (born 1946 to 1964) This demographic pig-in-the-python was created by the population explosion after the GIs of WWII returned home. They grew up in a time of prosperity and came of age during the Cold War and Vietnam. Unlike their parents, many became great consumers.

Generation X (born 1965 to 1981) First called Generation Bust because their birth rate was much smaller than the Baby Boomers, the term Generation X was popularized by

Douglas Coupland's 1991 novel ***Generation X: Tales For An Accelerated Culture***. They are the highest educated group to date.

Millennials (born 1982 to 2000) Originally called Generation Y, the name comes from the book ***Millennials Rising: The Next Generation*** by William Strauss and William Howe. Eighty million strong, they came of age in the Internet Revolution and now outnumber the Baby Boomers.

Generation Z (born 2001 to present) They'll come of age in a world of artificial intelligence and virtual reality and might end up being called Generation Tech, Generation Wired or Trons. We'll just have to wait and see.

Part I

Saving

"A penny Saved is twopence dear"
Poor Richard's Almanac
Benjamin Franklin

"…a foole and his money is soone parted."
John Bridges 1587

"This above all: to thine own self be true,
And it must follow as the night the day,
Thou canst not then be false to any man."
Polonius' advice to his son Laertes
Hamlet, Act I

"We have met the enemy and he is us."
Pogo (by Walt Kelly)

"I put myself on an allowance, and I'm probably one of the only guys from the seventies that still has cash."
Alice Cooper
Singer songwriter

"Whoever drinks beer, he is quick to sleep;
whoever sleeps long, does not sin;
whoever does not sin, enters Heaven.
Thus, let us all drink beer!"
Martin Luther

The Big Picture

"Capitalism is the astounding belief that the most wickedest of men will do the most wickedest of things for the greatest good of everyone."
John Maynard Keynes

A British dude named John Maynard Keynes was a big time economist in the last century. He wrote about a thing called the "Paradox of Thrift," which theorized that if individuals tried to save more during a recession it would decrease demand and consumption, stifle economic growth, and lead to greater unemployment, thereby actually decreasing the savings rate.

Mr. Keynes needn't worry about Americans today, because we are a consumption-driven society with an aversion toward savings. Boy, do we know how to spend money! But most of us don't know how to save, or how much to save, nor have clear savings goals, or a plan to achieve them. We have a glaring lack of financial literacy at a time when it's very important to be able to chart a course toward reaching one's financial goals.

In past generations, when people were much more self-reliant, security in old age was provided by the family. Over time, a government-provided safety net along with corporate pension plans made retirement much more secure. However, as we'll see, today those pensions have evolved, and *you* are now responsible for making the investment decisions that will determine how much money you end up with when you reach your "golden years." You are now the captain of your own retirement ship, so you had better learn something about $ailing.

There's a place in Murfreesboro, TN, called Deep South Growlers where you can buy a 64 ounce growler of beer to go, and when you're finished, you may bring the jug back and try another of their selection of craft brews. Of course you can have a pint or a sampler while you're trying to decide which one to take home. One thing I like about the place is that they have two root beers on tap: one regular and one "hard" with 7% alcohol. (I don't know why, but when I first saw that, a vision of Bill Murray coaching a Bad News Bears type team popped into my head, with Coach saying to the players after the big game, "Hey kids. I know a place that has the best root-beer in town. Wha'cha say we go try some?")

Realizing that for many, personal finance can be really boring stuff and make your eyes glaze over just a wee bit, I'll make this as short and sweet as I can. When you're done, or sooner if needed, you can treat yourself to a cold "root beer." If you're not into beer--of the root or any other kind--a glass of grape juice will suffice. Might I recommend one of the noble varietals such as Merlot or Chardonnay. Keep in mind that when I suggest an adult beverage, I don't mean you should get knee-walkin', commode-huggin' faced. I just figured that for some readers, a little liquid courage might be needed to get you started or to celebrate in the end.

Now let's begin.

The Risk Shift

Being the goodhearted people that they are, the Presbyterian Church created a fund for retired ministers way back in 1717. But most workers in those days were on their own when it came to any kind of financial support later in life, until the Social Security System was created in 1935.

A long time ago, before the earth cooled, and when television was only broadcast in black and white, there was a show called *The Waltons* that was set in rural Virginia in the 1930s,

---

Beer Pong With Paddles – The roots of modern Beer Pong can be found in Hanover, Hew Hampshire. Around 1955 some frat boys at Dartmouth College started playing "Beer Pong with Paddles" after some spectators reportedly set their cups on the ping pong table during a match. The college briefly sanctioned it as an intramural sport, before coming to their senses. (Dartmouth's mascot is officially Big Green but the unofficial mascot is Keggy the Keg, which leads me to believe there's not a lot to do in Hanover, but they do like their beer.)

In the 1970s students at Bucknell University and nearby Lehigh University in Pennsylvania played a version without paddles and called it "Throw Pong," which later became known as "Beirut" and eventually evolved into the Beer Pong played today. By the end of the century it had migrated all the way to the left coast and today is so popular that a World Series of Beer Pong is held in Las Vegas every year with teams from around the world and prize money in the tens of thousands of dollars. (Supposedly, at Utah State, where alcohol is not allowed on campus, the game is actually played using root-beer. Wink, wink.)

 and pretty much showed how most families took care of their own during that era. Extended families lived in the same household or in close proximity with three or more generations often under one roof. Parents took care of their children, and when the parents grew old, the children took care of them. With the advent of Social Security, a safety net was created beneath the fruits of a lifetime of labor.

Eventually, companies large and small began offering their own retirement plans which provided even more security, and the extended family created by necessity gradually gave way to the nuclear family of today. While Social Security was a godsend for millions, it was only intended to augment what workers had accumulated on their own. Retirement plans provided additional benefits and further enhanced the financial health of retirees. Many workers were able to get by quite comfortably on those two checks every month. However, nowadays these retirement plans have changed dramatically.

There are two basic types of retirement plans: Defined Benefit Plans and Defined Contribution Plans, with several offshoots and hybrids.

In the **Defined Benefit Plan**, workers receive a fixed monthly amount for life (the benefit) based on their earnings and years of service. Typically the formula is a percentage of final earnings times years of service. For example, say you're a professional Olympic swimmer like Michael Phelps. After 33 years (and 122 medals) of competition in the pool, you're waterlogged and decide to retire. With 2% of final average earnings of $100,000 you would receive 66% (2% x 33 years) of $100,000, or $66,000 annually. This plan was a mainstay for many years in corporate America and is still the norm for most federal, state, and municipal workers.

In the private sector, the Defined Benefit Plan has given way to the **Defined Contribution Plan**, often called a 401k after section 401k of the IRS code. In this type plan the employee can put money into an account (the contribution), which grows tax deferred. Then he or she gets whatever it grows to upon retirement. Unfortunately, employer contributions are not required, and since this is usually a self-directed investment account it may or may not meet your retirement goals, depending on the amount of your contributions and the success of your investment decisions. This is why it's important to have at least some understanding of the basics of investing.

ERISA

To explain how this change came about, a little history is in order. Early pension plans in the U.S. were very loosely regulated. In 1963, auto manufacturer Studebaker Corporation went out of business and many of its employees were left with nothing because the pension account was severely underfunded. This prompted pension reform efforts in Congress, and in 1974, the Employee Retirement Income Security Act (ERISA) was enacted, providing much needed stabilization in the industry and enhanced protections for workers and their Beneficiaries.

Under ERISA, corporate Defined Benefit Plans are taxed to provide insurance by the Pension Benefit Guarantee Corporation (PBGC) in case a company goes into bankruptcy or out of business. These extra costs, plus foreign competition, pushed the private sector toward Defined Contribution Plans which shifted risk away from employers and onto employees. In 1980, there were approximately 250,000 qualified Defined Benefit Plans, but today such plans have pretty much gone the way of the dinosaur.

The Studebaker brothers had been making wagons since 1852 in South Bend, Indiana, and in 1902 entered the horseless carriage business. Like many others, they started with electric vehicles, but by 1911, were building only gasoline models, and for the next 50 years Studebaker was known for high quality, reliable automobiles. During the depression they even introduced a low cost car called the Rockne, named after the legendary Notre Dame football coach, but folks weren't buying, and it was discontinued after two years.

In the early 1950s a price war between Ford and General Motors erupted, and smaller car companies like Studebaker couldn't keep up. A merger with Packard provided some short term relief, but by 1962 the handwriting was on the wall, and the last Studebaker rolled off the assembly line in 1966. Unfortunately for the 10,500 remaining workers, the pension fund was severely underfunded. The 3,600 employees who had reached retirement age received full pensions, while 4,000 workers between age 40 and 59 received 15% of their pensions, and the rest got nothing.

In 1937 Studebaker planted 5,000 trees to spell out the corporate name at their test facility about five miles south of New Carlisle, Indiana, which is 15 miles west of South Bend on US 20. Go to Google Earth and zoom in and you can still see the trees at the northwest corner of the track.

While Defined Benefit Plans provided a lot of certainty for workers, they meant uncertainty for the employers who had to increase or decrease the amount of money in the plan each year in response to economic conditions to meet obligations. On the other hand, Defined Contribution Plans provided certainty for the employer but uncertainty for the employee.

Let me explain this one more time to make sure you understand it. In the old days the company was guaranteeing the amount of your monthly check in retirement, unless they went out of business, in which case you were screwed. When the 401k came along, the employer didn't have to contribute to your retirement account, so the size of your monthly retirement check depended on how much you put in and the financial decisions you made. This is important to understand. If you don't put money into the account you get nothing back, and if you don't make wise financial decisions, you might not end up with as much money as you thought you would.

Yale professor Jacob Hacker wrote a book about this change aptly called **The Great Risk Shift**. This fundamental shift is why maximizing your savings and increasing your investing knowledge is so important for Millennials if you are to achieve the comfortable retirement you desire and save you from having to seek out a Walton family to take care of you.

One early problem with the switch to 401k plans was that employee participation was not mandatory. You know how that goes: "I'll sign up next month; I promise." It was an opt-in type system and many workers never got around to signing up. Plus, companies were not required to throw in any money. This was a double whammy, because as the country was moving away from Defined Benefit Plans, fewer workers were participating in 401k plans.

To correct this, in 2006, Congress changed the law and required employers to automatically

---

The Waltons – At the end of the 1971-1972 television season CBS (which had jokingly been nicknamed the Country Broadcasting System) concluded what became known as the "rural purge." Television shows such as The Beverly Hillbillies, Green Acres, and Hee Haw, joined previously canceled Mister Ed, The Andy Griffith Show, and Petticoat Junction on the scrapheap as the network switched to more urban-based sitcoms. Backlash to the rural purge and congressional hearings on the quality of television prompted CBS in 1972, to air *The Waltons*, a folksy drama based on Earl Hamner's book **Spencer Mountain**. They really didn't expect it to succeed and wanted to show Congress that America didn't care for rural based programming anymore. Ironically, *The Waltons* was a big success, ran for nine seasons, earned a Peabody Award, a Golden Globe and nine Emmys for its cast members, and spawned six feature-length movies for television. Reruns are still being aired today.

enroll workers, and allow them to opt-out if they so choose. The new law also established Safe Harbor 401k plans which allowed employers to automatically withhold an escalating amount of the employee's wages for investment into "target date" type funds (more on those later). For example, in the first year 3% would be withheld, year two 4%, etc., up to a maximum of 6%. Under Safe Harbor plans, companies were also required to match a portion of the employee's contributions, usually matching the first 3% of salary and then half of the contribution from 3% to 5%. This was a step in the right direction, but unfortunately these Safe Harbor plans were not mandatory for companies, and the legislation did nothing for those enrolled in plans created prior to 2006.

All you have to remember is this: if you find yourself working for an employer that has a plan with a company match, you're a fool not to participate. This is **free money**! It's an absolute no-brainier. Never pass up an employer's match!

IRAs

For those who are self-employed or working for companies without 401k plans, ERISA also created the Individual Retirement Account, or IRA. Today there are several types of IRAs but the two most common are the Traditional IRA and the Roth IRA.

The Traditional IRA was included in the original law and allows individuals to make pre-tax contributions to retirement accounts set up for the exclusive benefit of account holders and their beneficiaries. What this means is that if you earned $50,000 for the year and contributed $5,000 to your IRA, you would subtract the $5,000 from your taxable income and file your income taxes as if you had earned only $45,000. This is a good deal from Uncle Sam, not only because of the tax-free contributions, but because all the contributions grow tax free over time. However taxes must be paid on those dollars whenever you take money out. Withdrawals can be taken as early as age 59½, but since Uncle eventually must have his pound of flesh, required minimum distributions (RMD) must be taken after age 70½.

The IRA was the best thing to come along since some Dartmouth frat boys invented Beer Pong, but in 1997 an even better deal came out of Washington. The Roth IRA, named after Senator William Roth of Delaware, became the Chuck Norris of retirement investment vehicles, especially for Millennials. With a Roth IRA, the government gets its money up front, because account holders fund it with after-tax dollars. This means, in the above example, after putting in $5,000 you would file your tax return showing the full $50,000 as your earned income. The good news is that since Uncle already got his taxes, there are no required minimum distributions at age 70½. Because most workers are in a lower tax bracket when starting out, and the politicians in Washington spend money like drunken sailors, income taxes will likely be higher in future decades. This makes the Roth IRA a better choice for Millennials.

Of course you must have earned income (what's shown on a W-2 Form from an employer) to put money into any IRA, and there are income limits for contributing to a Roth or deducting contributions to a traditional IRA. There are maximum annual contribution limits too -- $5,500 per year for 2016. To clear up one misconception some people have about individual retirement accounts, remember that the A in IRA stands for "account." An IRA is not an investment unto itself, but merely an account into which you place investments.

Recognizing how hard stay-at-home spouses work, the law allows them to have an IRA even without any earned income. The rules are pretty simple. A married couple who files a joint tax return can each have an IRA provided the working spouse has earned income greater than the total amount contributed to the two accounts ($11,000 maximum).

Just because Defined Benefit Plans in the private sector have been replaced by Defined Contribution Plans, do not think that the workers of America have once again been "screwed by the system." There are a lot of positives to 401k type plans. For one, the money is yours and yours alone. All of your contributions, and after a short vesting period, all of the

---

Aunt Ida and Hilda – Our Social Security System was created in 1935, during the midst of the Great Depression. On 4 November 1939, sixty-five year old former school teacher Ida Mae Fuller, known as Aunt Ida to her friends, walked into the Rutland, Vermont Social Security office to ask about benefits. She had paid social security taxes totaling $24.75 over the previous three years, and hers became the first claim processed in Washington, DC. On 31 January 1940, Ida received check number 00-000-0001, in the amount of $22.54. She lived to be 100 years of age and collected $22,888.92 in benefits during her lifetime. Not a bad return on her investment.

Of the more than 450 million social security numbers issued to date, the most famous one is 078-05-0112. In 1938, a wallet manufacturer in Lockport, New York decided to enclose a sample social security card in its wallets to highlight the wallet's features. An executive copied the card of his secretary, Hilda Schrader Witcher for the promotion. Even though the sample card was printed in red, had the word "specimen" across the front, and was half the size of a real card, many purchasers of the wallet took the number as their own. By 1943, more than 5,750 people were using Hilda's SSN. She was issued a new card, but over the years more than 40,000 people used her old number with a dozen still doing so as late as 1977.

employer's contributions, if any, are protected from creditors should the company go into bankruptcy or out of business. That's a big deal. As mentioned earlier, many Studebaker workers were left with nothing. Even though the PBGC now insures traditional pensions, workers only receive a fraction of what they would have gotten had the company remained solvent.

Today, even many state and municipal Defined Benefit Plans are under pressure due to under-performing assets and governments promising more than they can deliver. In Detroit's bankruptcy in 2013, retired workers had their benefits reduced and current workers will see less in the future. The only ones who are safe for now are federal employees, since the U.S. government owns the printing presses and can crank out as many greenbacks as they need.

The greatest advantage, and risk, of a Defined Contribution Plan and IRA is that you are now in charge of how your money is invested. With a little knowledge and self-discipline, you can grow it into a tidy nest egg or, as we'll see, you can miss out on a lot of potential gains.

Hopefully that wasn't too boring, and you now have a little better understanding of the retirement landscape. Well done! Go pour that much-deserved beverage of your choice.

Mom, Baseball, Apple Pie, and Debt

We Americans, as a nation, are poor savers relative to other countries of the world. The CIA's *World Factbook* includes a country by country comparison of gross national savings as a percentage of Gross Domestic product (GDP). The United States is ranked 99th. In so-called emerging markets, most people save out of necessity due to the lack of a transparent banking system and minimal social safety nets such as unemployment insurance, retirement plans, and health care. Even an economic giant like China, with its growing consumerism, hangs on to its conservative saving habit.

So what happened in America, the home of the thrifty New Englander, Ben Franklin and *Poor Richard's Almanac*? Some would argue that our social safety nets and retirement plans provide less incentive for Americans to save. If that logic were true, one might assume that in the liberal welfare states of Europe, with their cradle-to-grave government programs, savings rates would be even lower than here at home, especially in socialistic Scandinavia. Turns out that's not the case. Most European countries save a greater percentage of their GDP than we do. Only Portugal, Greece and the United Kingdom lag behind the United States.

We weren't always a nation of lousy savers. Historically our individual household savings rate--as opposed to the national percentage of GDP--was pretty good. We were fair, if not great savers, and always stepped up to the plate in times of crisis. In ***Beyond Our Means: Why Americans Spend While the World Saves***, Princeton professor Sheldon Garon says that a lot of our current predicament has to do with government actions that originally encouraged savings, then later discouraged it and promoted consumption.

In 1910, the Postal Savings System was established in select U.S. Post Offices around the country to get money out from under the mattresses of immigrants who were accustomed to saving at post offices in their native countries, and to provide safety for Americans who had little confidence in banks. The system was based on one established by the British to promote savings among the poor. Unlike private banks, deposits of any size were accepted, fees were low, and the accounts were backed by the government. However, with the creation of the Federal Deposit Insurance Corporation (FDIC) in 1933, this advantage was lost, and by 1966, the system was discontinued. While in effect, it did encourage the poorest Americans to save. Maybe it's something we should look into again.

> **First, Second and Third** – The talking heads on the idiot tube used to talk about the "third world" a lot. Did you ever wonder where the term came from?
>
> Prior to the French Revolution historians referred to the church as the First Estate, nobility as the Second Estate, and all the lower classes of society as the Third Estate. (Later, in the 19th century, the term Fourth Estate was used to refer to the press.) In 1952, French demographer Alfred Sauvy coined the term Third World in an article titled: "That Third World, Ignored, Exploited, Scorned, Like the Third Estate."
>
> By the late 1960s, the term was in common use in the English speaking world, and by extension the terms First World and Second World were applied to the two sides involved in the Cold War: First World for the democratic, industrialized countries of the West, and Second World for the communist nations that were east of the Iron Curtain. Later in the Cold War, the Third World countries attempted to ban together as the "non-aligned" nations to mitigate the influence and exploitation of the East and West. Usage of the term died with the Cold War and today "lesser developed nations" or "emerging markets" are used, more in an economic rather than a geopolitical sense.

Besides using the Postal Savings System, many middle and lower income Americans saved by buying savings bonds. Born during the depression, a savings bond was the only way ordinary citizens could afford to buy fixed rate government bonds. During World War II they were called "war savings bonds" and buying them was considered a patriotic duty. For $18.75 anyone could buy a $25 face value bond and cash it in after a fixed number of years. Kids in schools would buy 25 cent savings stamps to stick in booklets that held 75 stamps each, and once a booklet was filled it could be redeemed for a bond.

South Dakota Saves Citibank

Before credit cards you could only spend what was in your wallet or bank account. In 1958, Bank of America launched the first general purpose credit card using mass mailings to hundreds of thousands of people across the country in order to cash in on the post WWII consumer spending boom. This new "revolving credit" could be used anywhere and paid off at your convenience. Soon, other banks were in the game and competing for new Customers.

For the first decade, the banks made little money, primarily because state usury laws limited how much interest could be charged. Then in 1978, the Supreme Court ruled that banks could export the usury laws of their home state throughout the country. This opened the credit card floodgates.

In the midst of a recession in 1980, New York-based Citibank was losing money because state usury laws in New York were forcing them to lend money for less than the rate of inflation. Walter Wristen, the CEO of Citibank, tried to convince the politicians in Albany to change the usury rate to no avail, so he went looking for a new home. But the new Federal law would not allow banks to set up operations in other states unless they were invited into that state by the legislature.

About the same time, the recession was wreaking havoc on the economy of South Dakota. Unemployment was high, and Governor Bill Janklow was in the midst of eliminating his state's usury laws in hopes of bringing jobs to the state. When Walter Wristen called the governor offering to relocate Citibank to South Dakota, it was a match made in heaven. The legislation inviting Citibank in was introduced and passed in one day and eventually brought more than 3,000 good jobs to the state.

Banks across the country began calling, and South Dakota had visions of becoming the financial center of America. Unfortunately, these hopes were dashed when the Delaware legislature quickly followed suit and corralled a large share of the credit card business. During the 1980s, the number of credit cards doubled, balances increased five-fold, and profits for the banks soared. We were well on our way to becoming "big spenders" and living beyond our means.

Other events came along to give banks a financial boost and make it easier for Americans to go into debt. During the 1980 recession, President Carter put a freeze on new credit card solicitations in an effort to slow inflation. This provided an opportunity for the banks to introduce a new feature on their credit cards: the $20 annual fee. Because of the freeze, defections were minimal, and the banks found a huge new source of revenue.

Later, rising home values in the 1990s brought the home equity line of credit (HELOC) to the forefront. Equity is the value of the home above the balance of the mortgage. These

---

Usury – In modern law, usury refers to lending money at unreasonable interest rates. As far back as ancient Greece and Rome, men such as Aristotle and Cato condemned the charging of any interest, and in most religions it was considered an immoral exploitation of the poor. For the Jews however, Deuteronomy 23:20 allowed "Unto a stranger thou mayest lend upon usury; but unto thy brother thou shalt not lend upon usury…" which was interpreted to mean they could not charge interest of a fellow Israelite but could charge others.

Over time the Jews became the bankers of Western civilization and it gave them power and influence way out of proportion to their numbers which led to jealousy and horrendous persecution. During the twelfth and thirteenth centuries, one third of the Jews of Europe were murdered by crusaders en route to the Holy Land, and throughout the Middle Ages the "usurious Jews" were expelled from countless towns and villages. They even became scapegoats for the Black Death. By the time Henry VIII allowed interest of up to 10% to be charged in 1545, antisemitism was firmly entrenched throughout much of the world and continues to this day. It's amazing how the interpretation of a single word has led to so much senseless death and destruction.

variable interest rate HELOCs allowed homeowners to spend the equity they had in their homes, and to make it even more enticing, the government made the interest paid on these loans tax-deductible. By the turn of the century, we were spending like drunken sailors.

One last word about banks and credit card companies. Banks love cardholders who carry a balance from month to month and call them "revolvers." With today's high interest rates on cards, it's a big money maker. Those who pay off their balance every month don't make the banks any money and are referred to as "deadbeats." Always strive to be a deadbeat.

Know Thyself

Let's not place all the blame on the government because we're poor savers. After all, there are many Americans who save regularly. Maybe it's just in our nature, and at least for some of us, it is. There's an age-old debate about nature verses nurture. The nurture side of the argument says that we are born with a clean slate, and who we are or what we become is a product of our environment. The nature side contends we are genetically pre-wired at birth as to what type person we will eventually be. The answer, of course, is we're a mixture of both.

Neurological research does shed some light on the workings of our brains when it comes to money. In an article in *The Journal of Consumer Research*, titled "Tightwads and Spendthrifts," researchers Scott I. Rick, Cynthia E. Cryder, and George Lowenstein concluded that 60% of us are not conflicted by money. However, after interviewing more than 13,000 people, the researchers reported that 24% of respondents were tightwads, and 16% were spendthrifts. Using functional MRI, they discovered that most subjects, when shown pictures of desirable things such as chocolate, the *nucleus accumbens*, or pleasure center of the brain, showed increased activity. But when subjects saw the price tag for the chocolate, the *insular cortex*, or disgust center of the brain, showed increased activity. The pain of having to pay for the chocolate seems to mitigate the desire for pleasure.

However, in spendthrifts, the pain of spending didn't register much if at all, and for tightwads the anguish of spending was so strong it seemed to override rational desire. Gender plays a role too, with males being three times more likely to be tightwads than females, while income levels had no effect.

As you may have guessed, they found a large spending gap between tightwads and spendthrifts when it came to using cash, but virtually none when it came to using credit cards, further demonstrating that it's difficult for many of us to pull money out of our wallets and way too easy for everyone to use plastic.

So what is this "know thyself" stuff? It might sound like some kind of weird psycho-babble but, as I said in the introduction, you first must know what type of person you are, or you could spend your life being your own worst enemy. When it comes to money, and a lot of other aspects of life, your personal behavior determines how much success you'll have in reaching your goals. If who you are is not conducive to a healthy, happy and productive life, you'll have to make changes.

There's a plethora of professional help available for people with weight, drug, alcohol, gambling, and a myriad of other behavioral problems; the initial step toward change is always to first realize there is a problem. It's the same thing when it comes to fiscal health.

So sit down, look in the mirror and ask yourself: Who am I? Perusing your credit card statement or that shoe-box full of receipts buried in the desk may help give you an idea. How much are you spending on entertainment, eating out, vacations, and other things that you might not be able to afford? Does money burn a hole in your pocket? Are you spending a lot paying down debt? How much do you have in savings?

Next, get a second opinion. Ask close friends and family how they view your fiscal habits because you might need their help setting goals and developing a plan to change.

> **ADD and Subtract** – In the nineties it seemed that every class my boys were in had at least one student on Ritalin, and I carped as much as anyone about giving stimulants to kids that couldn't sit still. Of course, I didn't know what I was talking about or how much ADD really can subtract from your life. Turns out the prefrontal cortex has what's called executive function over other parts of the brain that relate to forethought, judgment, planning, impulse control, and managing money, and it needs to be stimulated to do its job.
>
> About 6-7% of people are affected worldwide and 75% of cases are inherited. Boys are three times more likely to be diagnosed than girls. The bad news is that about half of those with ADD abuse drugs/alcohol, and have higher rates of incarceration, obesity, depression, divorce, and even Alzheimer's. They do and say things without thinking and are often spendthrifts. The good news is that they are usually creative, intelligent, spontaneous, and great at thinking outside the box. They make good writers, sales people, artists, and CEO's and are over-represented among firefighters and emergency room doctors because they crave stimulation and challenges. A few people you may have heard of that suffer from ADD include Michael Phelps, Adam Levine, Justin Timberlake, Glen Beck, Richard Branson, Ryan Gosling, Virgil Green, Terry Bradshaw, Jason Kidd, Magic Johnson, Barry Pencek and Will Smith.

In the spring of 1971 I purchased a brand new Volkswagen Type 3 Fastback. I bought the car because it was inexpensive and reliable. I kept the car for 13 years for another reason: it was limiting. That little VW would top out at 85 miles per hour, but only downhill with a tailwind. I knew that if I had a car that could go 120 miles an hour, I would have tried it and probably wrapped it around a tree. I just didn't have the self-control to own a faster car.

Likewise with spendthrifts, if you don't have the self-discipline to hold on to your cash, you're going to have to come up with strategies to impose limits, like restricting access to your accounts or even, in extreme cases, having someone else control your money.

Spendthrifts and Frugalers

Just for the sake of discussion and illustration let's say the brain changes noted in people who over-spend and under-spend are due to genetics. Who knows, maybe genes do play a part. I'm hypothetically looking at five genes, let's call them A, B, C, D, & E and they look something like this.

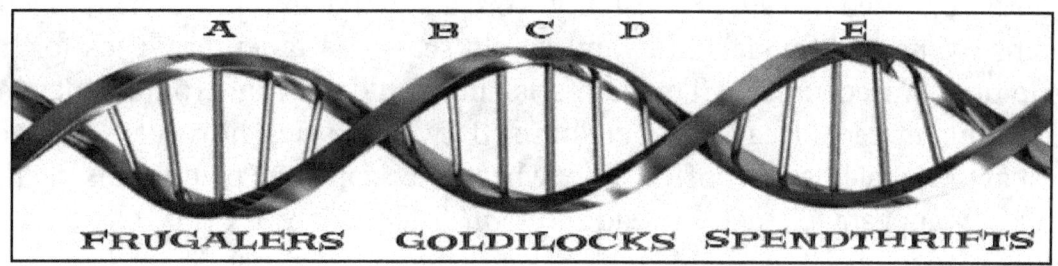

A. I call them frugalers. Yeah I know, there's no such word, but the term tightwad seems much too negative for my liking. For the 24% born with the A gene it's painful to spend. I suppose they could easily become misers or hoarders and may live mundane lives. A bit over the top, one might say.

B. They clip coupons, buy most things on sale and usually pay cash or save money for a hefty down payment before making large purchases. Saving is pleasurable. I can relate to these folks.

C. Goldilocks are kind of like the nursery story: not too tight, not too loose—just right.

D. They have to be careful separating wants from needs and must be disciplined in their savings. "Pay Yourself First" needs to be their mantra. (More on that later.)

E. Spendthrifts are the U. S. Congress types: give them a dollar and they'll spend a buck and a quarter; and they make up about 16% of the population. Because the government can print money, it can get by with this for quite some time, but do it in your personal life and you're on the road to ruin.

When it comes to saving, how much money you earn is not necessarily relevant. If you're a frugaler, you can't help but salt away money, but if you're a spendthrift, you most likely won't save unless you muster a whole lot of self-discipline.

Here's a whale of an example of a spendthrift: I had a squadron-mate back in the 70s who got out of the Marines and was well on his way to being a very successful stockbroker. I was surprised when he told me he had clients making over $500,000 a year (a ton of money back then) whose investment goals were to generate more income because they "couldn't make ends meet." They just weren't savers, and no matter how much money they earned they would always need more.

> **Frugalers** – Ronald Read was known around Brattleboro, Vermont, as a private and unassuming man. After serving in the Army in World War II, he took a job as a service station attendant and mechanic until the garage closed, then worked as a janitor at J. C. Penny until he retired in 1997. He usually wore a khaki denim jacket held together with safety pins over worn flannel shirts and would scavenge fallen branches for his wood stove. He drove a secondhand Toyota Yaris and would park far from his destination to avoid parking meters. Read allowed himself two luxuries however: He would eat breakfast at the local hospital coffee shop, where once someone paid for his meal because of his scruffy appearance, and he read the *Wall Street Journal* every day at the library. Ronald Read died on 2 June 2014, and left an estate of more than $8 million. Among his bequeaths was $4.8 million to the Brattleboro Memorial Hospital and $1.2 million to the Brooks Memorial Library.
>
> Anne Scheiber lived in a rent-controlled, rundown apartment in New York City, worked as an auditor for the IRS, and usually wore the same black coat and hat wherever she went. She never made more than $4,000 a year, never married, never went out, and walked everywhere because she never owned a car. After 23 years with the IRS, having never gotten a promotion and feeling like she was often discriminated against, she retired in 1944 with a $3,100 pension, and $5,000 in savings. She devoted the next 50 years to investing and parlayed her meager savings into an estate of more than $22 million but continued to live in the same apartment and walked about in the same old clothes. It's said she once took enough food from a shareholders meeting buffet to eat for three days. When she died in 1995 at age 101, she left the majority of her estate to Yeshiva

On the other end of the spectrum there are outliers who are beyond being frugalars and truly deserve to be called tightwads or cheapskates. Billionaire oilman J. Paul Getty was such a person. It's said he installed a pay telephone in his London home so guests wouldn't make long-distance calls at his expense, and when his 16-year-old grandson was kidnapped he refused to pay the $17 million ransom. Only after the kidnappers mailed him his grandson's ear did he pay the ransom, but not before negotiating the price down to $3.4 million. What a grandfather!

According to the Rick, Cryder and Lowenstein research, it looks like the majority of us are going to be all right when it comes to the psychology of handling money, but the Frugalers and Spendthrifts need some assistance. Here are a few guidelines that may help:

Frugalers
    Always have separate accounts for spending and saving;
    Set up a "fun" account that you must spend on vacations, going out and having fun;
    Use credit cards instead of cash;
    Be proud that you're a "deadbeat" and the banks hate you;
    If you win the lottery, take the lump sum.

Spendthrifts
    A written budget is mandatory;
    Use debit cards and avoid credit. Cash is even better;
    Never use plastic, even debit cards, for purchases under $20. This will drastically reduce spending on frivolous items.
    Payroll deductions and automatic bank transfers are your friend;
    Set up separate accounts for each savings goal—never commingle funds;
    Make your money less accessible by not signing up for online banking;
    If you win the lottery, take the 30 year annuity.

Barry Pencek

Uncle Dick and Uncle Trev

People toward the frugaler end of the spectrum are usually interested in, and enjoy saving and growing money, while for those toward the opposite end it may be an afterthought, if that. Here's what I mean: Growing up I had two uncles who were brothers, yet as is normal, they had some differences. Both were intelligent men with doctorate degrees who spent their careers in education, one as a public school administrator in the East and the other as a university professor in the Midwest. Both were family men well respected in their communities.

Uncle Trev (short for Trever, which got changed from the traditional Welsh spelling "Trevor" when my great-grandfather came through Ellis Island) was almost a frugaler and enjoyed investing. I visited with him when he was well into his eighties, and he still liked to talk about money, the stock market, investing and the economy.

Uncle Dick was more of a spendthrift and had little interest in anything financial. Later in life he told me that he wished he knew more about it and had made some different financial

---

Minnesota Twins – This is not about a baseball team but rather studies of twins in Minnesota. Researchers there have been studying twins since 1883, when the Minnesota Twin Registry was established for psychological research. In 1979, University of Minnesota professor Dr. Thomas Bouchard launched a study of identical and fraternal twins from around the world, who were separated at birth and reared apart, to examine what degree of similarities between twins was due to environment (nurture) and how much was due to genes (nature). After studying more than 100 sets of twins (and some triplets) Bouchard determined that for identical twins, whether reared apart or together, there was a strong correlation in IQ, personality, temperament, and leisure time interests, but lesser correlation when it came to religion, social attitudes and political views. Some of the twins studied were interesting to say the least. For example:

- Barbara Herbert and Daphne Goodship (reunited at age 40) discovered they sometimes cooked the same meal from the same cookbook on the same day, that they each had a miscarriage in the same year and then gave birth to two sons followed by one daughter.
- Tom Patterson was raised a Christian in Kansas and his twin, Steve Tazumi, was raised a Buddhist in New Jersey. Yet when they were reunited at age 39, they discovered they were both competitive power lifters and once owned bodybuilding gyms.

decisions earlier in life. I'll have to admit that upon hearing this, my initial reaction was one of shock. After all, every newspaper has a business section, financial books and magazines abound, and the internet has put all the financial information one could possibly want at our fingertips. How could you possibly not know about this stuff?

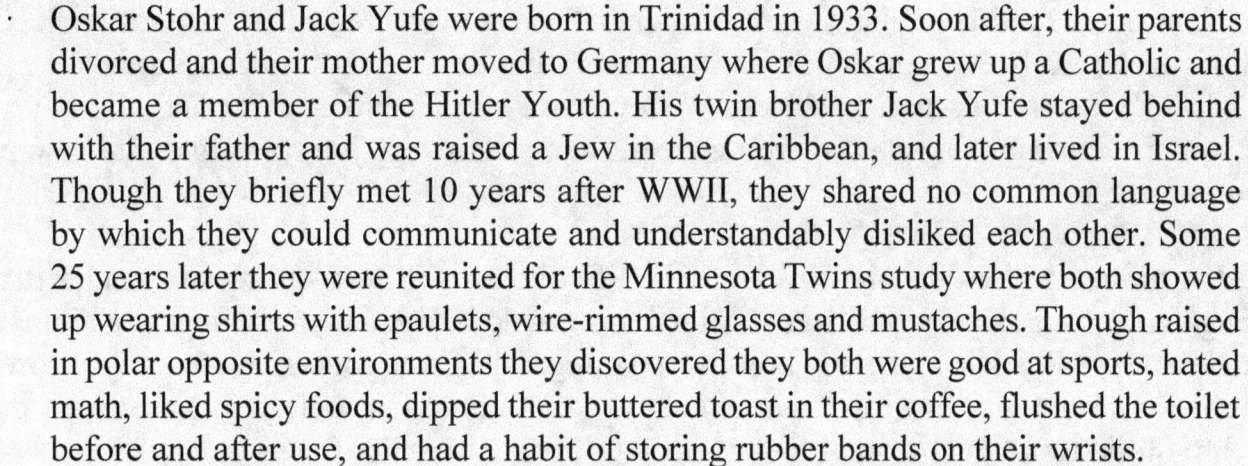

But I completely missed the point: we all have individual likes and dislikes and it's only human to focus on what we enjoy and tune out other things. For example, without a doubt, I am a pop culture idiot. When we play trivia on Monday nights at Johnny's Pizza, everyone on our team (the Nads) can't believe I don't have a clue who this movie star or that famous entertainer is. After all, they're all over the newspaper, television and internet. But I'm just not interested in that stuff, and I tune it out. I'd rather watch grass grow than pick up a copy of *People* magazine. The takeaway is that not knowing Bono from Bozo won't affect my quality of life, other than rendering me a pop culture dimwit at trivia, but not having some discipline and a basic grasp of a few financial principles can dramatically affect one's future.

- Oskar Stohr and Jack Yufe were born in Trinidad in 1933. Soon after, their parents divorced and their mother moved to Germany where Oskar grew up a Catholic and became a member of the Hitler Youth. His twin brother Jack Yufe stayed behind with their father and was raised a Jew in the Caribbean, and later lived in Israel. Though they briefly met 10 years after WWII, they shared no common language by which they could communicate and understandably disliked each other. Some 25 years later they were reunited for the Minnesota Twins study where both showed up wearing shirts with epaulets, wire-rimmed glasses and mustaches. Though raised in polar opposite environments they discovered they both were good at sports, hated math, liked spicy foods, dipped their buttered toast in their coffee, flushed the toilet before and after use, and had a habit of storing rubber bands on their wrists.
- James Springer and James Lewis were separated at one month of age, grew up in rural Ohio and were called Jim by their adoptive parents. When they were reunited at age 39 they discovered they each had married women named Linda, divorced, and remarried women named Betty. One had a son named James Allan while the other named his son James Alan, and both had dogs named Toy. They suffered from migraine headaches, chain smoked Salem cigarettes, drank Miller beer, bit their nails, drove Chevys and vacationed at the same beach in Florida. Each had served as deputy sheriffs in counties 45 miles apart, enjoyed woodworking in workshops in their garages, and had built white benches around trees in their backyards. Now that's crazy!

Uncle Dick was not an outlier of his generation and today's Millennials are similar in many ways. A Wells Fargo Millennial Study shows that 80% of Millennials claim the Great Recession taught them that they must save "now" for the future, yet 56% are living paycheck-to-paycheck, 39% say they are "overwhelmed with debt," and only 55% are saving for retirement. Yet, God bless them, they are overwhelmingly optimistic about the future, with 69% feeling they are better off than other Millennials and 68% expecting their standard of living to be better than their parents. At least I like their positive attitude. There are a lot of other mixed signals in the Wells Fargo study. For example:

– Almost half of Millennials are devoting more than 50% of their income to pay off debt;
– 77% believe they have the knowledge to address their financial problems;
– 67% participate in 401k's but only 46% have IRAs;
– Women are less hopeful about their finances and only 50% have begun saving for retirement.

Other research indicates that, compared to previous generations, Millennials are more narcissistic; have poor financial literacy; go to church less; consider wealth an important attribute; are less interested in politics but have strong civic values; socialize more; seek adventure; text—a lot (80% have a cell phone next to them when they sleep); rely on institutions less but network with friends more; and get along with their parents. Because of their unique attitudes about work, Millennials have even created an "aspiration gap" in the workforce. They want fulfillment from work but don't want it to consume their lives. Only 11% aspire to senior positions. With Generation X being smaller and ten thousand Boomers retiring every day, there's concern about an executive talent gap at the top in coming years.

I don't know if there is any way to predict if children will turn out to be spendthrifts or frugalers or somewhere in between. All parents can do is teach them about personal finance and hope it will stick. When my boys were young kids, I was concerned about the growing need for instant gratification that seemed to be taking hold in society so I presented them with a little test. One by one I took them into the pantry and offered them one candy bar (left over from Halloween, I'm sure) immediately, or they could wait half an hour and I would give them two candy bars. It cheered the cockles of my heart when each of them decided to wait and get two. I thought for sure the boys would be thrifty fellows when they grew up. Not so fast Kemosabe! Turns out my little test wasn't a real good predictor. One son leans toward being a frugaler, one toward being a spendthrift, one in the middle and the jury is still out on the fourth. You just never know how they're going to turn out.

Later, when they were teenagers, I offered them each $100 to read ***The Wealthy Barber*** by David Chilton. It is an entertaining story set in a barbershop where three young adults get a primer on financial planning from Tom, the local barber. Since the story was geared toward a younger audience and included some humorous banter about baseball, I thought my boys would find it an enjoyable read and leap at the chance to pick up some money. I figured I could slip in a little financial education, and they would be none the wiser. Two read the book and two didn't. Go figure! My last hope is that all of them will read this book. (Just had a bright idea. Maybe I'll insert each of their names in random places in the following pages, and if they find them, I'll know they read it.)

Pay Yourself First

It's been around for years and is often called the golden rule of personal finance, but "Pay Yourself First" is still sage advice in today's world. It simply means that before you pay your rent, before you buy groceries, before you pay bills, before you spend any of your paycheck on anything, you put money aside for savings. For frugalers it comes naturally, but if you're a spendthrift here's how it usually plays out: It's payday and you lay out money for rent/mortgage, car payment, insurance, utility bills, food, and a few nights out, and save what's left over. The problem is there's nothing left over. So you get a raise or a better paying job, get paid and pay the bills, go out, and again there's nothing left over to save. No matter how much money you earn you're still living paycheck to paycheck. It's like you're stuck in a *Ground Hog Day* scenario with very little to show for it year after year.

So how do you get there if saving doesn't come naturally? All hope is not lost, but you're going to need some discipline and make it automatic, painless, and invisible. A great little book is **The Automatic Millionaire** by David Bach, the premise of which is exactly that. The book opens with an interview with a fictional, middle-aged, blue-collared couple who have a net worth of several million dollars. They proceed to tell Bach, a financial planner, how when they were young, they set up payroll deductions and automatic bank transfers for retirement accounts, mortgage payments (plus extra to pay off the loan sooner), and savings accounts.

That's exactly what a spendthrift needs to do. You have to pay yourself first, before the money gets to your pocket and burns a hole in it. You won't miss what you don't see, and you won't see it if you set up automatic deductions. Over time, and with some prudent investing, these savings will grow.

If you want to really put your savings on steroids, every time you get a raise, put half of the increase in an investment account. You'll still get a raise, just half of what the boss gave you. If you get anything out of this section of the book, it has to be to Pay Yourself First, or you will never break the cycle of living paycheck-to-paycheck.

Barry Pencek

Write It Down

Most people respond better to seeing something in front of them in black and white, instead of a fuzzy notion in the back of their head, so it helps to write things down. The first item you'll need is a budget to see how much money is coming in and how much is going out, with a goal of always spending less than you earn. A written budget can be as simple as a sheet of paper with a line down the center showing income on the left and expenses on the right. Or it can be a computer spreadsheet that you create, or one of the dozens of online programs linked to your bank accounts with detailed data on your spending and instant access on a smart phone.

The point of having a written budget is that it brings clarity and allows you to see where your money is going, which helps you prioritize your spending. The income side of the ledger is usually pretty cut and dried, unless you're in commission sales, but the spending side needs to be more in depth. The more detailed, the better. Some obvious priority items are savings (pay yourself first), food, shelter, transportation, and insurance, but remember that there's a lot of leeway in these items. On the left is a sample budget, but you'll want to tailor yours to your own situation. The first time you do it you'll just have to take a stab at an amount for each category, then fine tune it over a few months. At the end of each month check your spending to see if you're over or under budget. If you're under budget give yourself a root beer, and if you're over budget go back to the drawing-board and sharpen your pencil. The most important thing is to spend less than you bring in.

INCOME	Budgeted Amt	Actual Amt	Difference
Wages and bonuses			
Miscellaneous			
Total Income			
EXPENSES			
Rent/Mortgage			
Food/Groceries			
Emergency Fund/IRA			
Water and Sewer			
Gas			
Electric			
Cable/Internet			
Phone			
Home/Renter's Insurance			
Auto Insurance			
Auto Loan			
Auto Exp. (gas, maint, tags, tolls.)			
Medical Expenses			
Credit Card Debt			
Student Loan			
Charity/Gifts			
Entertainment (dining out, movies.)			
Vacation Fund			
Pets			
Miscellaneous			
Total Expenses			

If you're not a natural saver, sorting out wants from needs becomes critical, or it will kill your budget. Let's say your old jalopy gives up the ghost and you go looking for replacement transportation. You *need* transportation to get to work, but you *want* that new Tesla Model S P100D that goes zero to sixty in 2.5 seconds and has leather everything, especially after the sales person says it's only a few hundred bucks a month if you finance it for the rest of your life. Besides, think of all the gas you won't have to buy with an electric car, and you get a tax credit, too. Wow, what a deal! And the list goes on.

There's a big difference between dining out and eating in, or living in the penthouse versus the basement flat. A written budget allows you to see where the money's going. If you're using an online budgeting tool, you can instantly see how much you're spending and perhaps get a much-needed kick in the pants when you discover how much you've been blowing on wants instead of needs.

In a survey of families with household income over $75,000 pollsters found that far too many are not saving. One third of the families surveyed were living paycheck to paycheck and 44 percent said that dining out and entertainment spending prevented them from saving more. For Millennials, that number was an astounding 71 percent. It seems like y'all are destined to dine out and party till the debt collectors come calling, then I suppose wonder what went wrong.

After completing your budget you need to establish your financial goals and write them down, too. To begin, you'll need a separate plan for each goal. These aren't elaborate documents and can be just a few lines on a sheet of paper. For example: Save $5,000 in two years toward a new car; put away $10,000 for an emergency fund within one year; accumulate $50,000 over the next five years for a down payment on a house; grow your

---

The O'Malley's – The Spendthrift and Fruglar genes are distributed without regard to social status, income or education. Here's a case in point: Katie Curran and Martin O'Malley met in law school, got married in 1990, and had four children. She pursued a career in law, becoming a District Court judge in Baltimore earning $141,000 a year while he went into politics and was elected mayor of Baltimore in 1999. In 2007 he was elected governor of Maryland which provided an annual salary of $150,000. Their attractive salaries were augmented by a pension of $61,000 from the city of Baltimore.

Public records showed the O'Malleys lived comfortably but had virtually no savings. They sent their children to private schools and when it came time for college, the O'Malleys took out $339,000 in education loans to send the eldest two kids to prestigious universities – the younger two are still in high school but will be ready for college soon. The family has faced some criticism for setting a poor example and not choosing a more affordable education for their children such as a public college in Maryland. *Ya think?*

IRA to $1 million over the next 40 years. Next, on the same page as each goal, put down how much you'll need to reach it. Use an online savings calculator (**dinkytown.net** or **bankrate.com**) to figure it out. Five grand in two years is $215 a month; ten thousand in one year is about $830 per month; and $50,000 over five years is $750 a month. "Whoa," you say. "I'm just out of school, starting a new job, and I'm supposed to save almost $1,800 every month! How about rent, and food, and root beer?" That's another thing that's great about putting numbers in front of you, it gives you a reality check and helps you prioritize.

As we'll see later, the investment strategy for each goal will be driven by the time horizon for whatever you're saving for, so you'll need separate accounts for saving for a new car, a down payment on a house, saving for a child's education and for your retirement. Also, by not commingling funds it will reduce the temptation to dip into long range accounts for short term needs, and you can better see how you're doing as far as reaching each individual goal. Early in marriage, Mary and I used what we came to call "teapot budgeting." We budgeted a set amount of money for groceries each month and put the cash in an old teapot on top of the refrigerator. Sometimes it was empty by the 25th of the month and we just had to be creative with what was in the refrigerator, garden and pantry, even though there might have been money in the checking account. It worked for us.

Now that you have a budget, established your goals, and set up your short term and long term savings accounts, just how much money should you be saving?

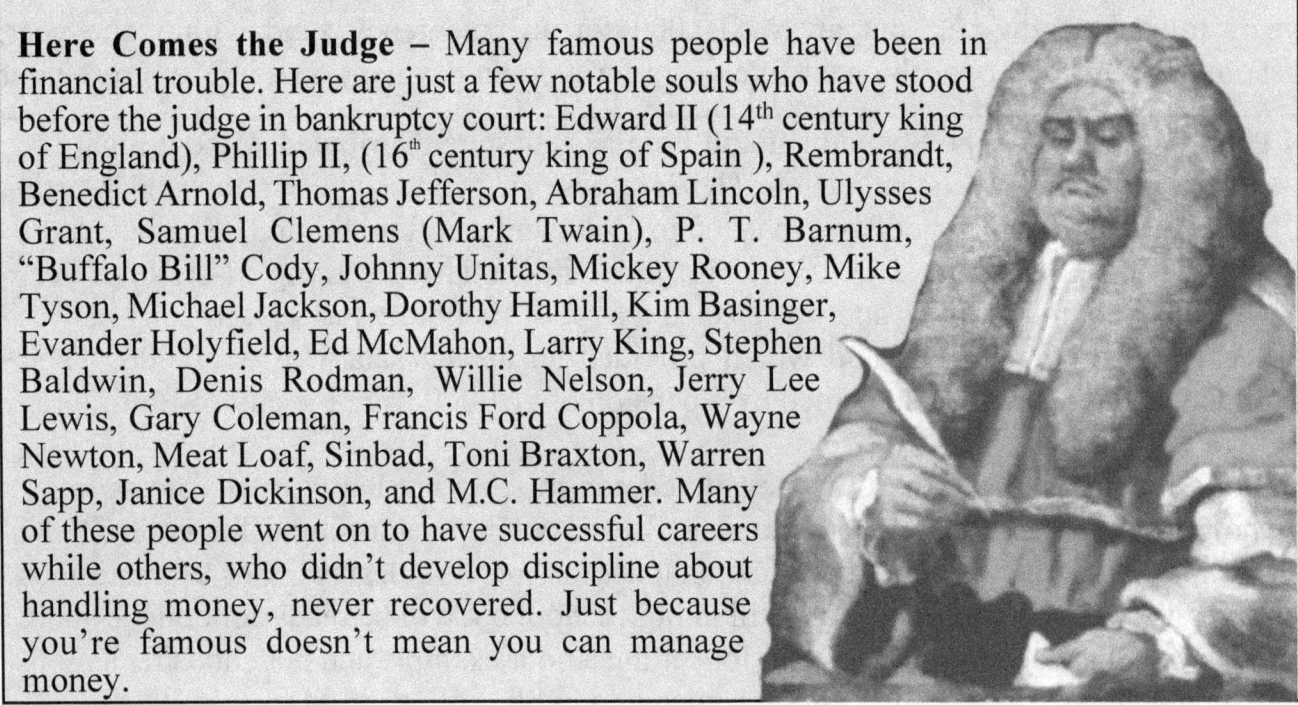

Here Comes the Judge – Many famous people have been in financial trouble. Here are just a few notable souls who have stood before the judge in bankruptcy court: Edward II (14th century king of England), Phillip II, (16th century king of Spain), Rembrandt, Benedict Arnold, Thomas Jefferson, Abraham Lincoln, Ulysses Grant, Samuel Clemens (Mark Twain), P. T. Barnum, "Buffalo Bill" Cody, Johnny Unitas, Mickey Rooney, Mike Tyson, Michael Jackson, Dorothy Hamill, Kim Basinger, Evander Holyfield, Ed McMahon, Larry King, Stephen Baldwin, Denis Rodman, Willie Nelson, Jerry Lee Lewis, Gary Coleman, Francis Ford Coppola, Wayne Newton, Meat Loaf, Sinbad, Toni Braxton, Warren Sapp, Janice Dickinson, and M.C. Hammer. Many of these people went on to have successful careers while others, who didn't develop discipline about handling money, never recovered. Just because you're famous doesn't mean you can manage money.

The Emergency Fund

Picture this: You pull up at the Kallikak Family Deli to get a pickled herring sandwich for lunch just as the circus parade hits Main Street. Before you even get out of your car, a rhinoceros breaks loose from the trainer, rampages down Main Street, and runs into your car. You end up with a totaled vehicle and a broken leg to boot, and can't go back to work. You're in trouble. Okay, so the rhinoceros is preposterous, but what if the transmission falls out of your car (a month after the warranty expires, of course) and you need it for work? Or how about you get downsized out of your job right after you signed the mortgage for a new house? If you don't have a cash stash, you're screwed. Grandma always said to save a little something for a rainy day, and she was right.

The very first thing you need to save for, and I mean the *very* first thing, is an emergency fund equal to around three to six months' living expenses. So, which is it you wonder—three months or six months? After all, one is twice as much as the other. Well, it depends on the circumstances. If you are single, just out of school, living at home, and driving that old paid up clunker, then three months is more than enough, and you might get by with less, depending on the largess of mom and dad. However, if you have a family and are the sole breadwinner with a mortgage, car payments, food, clothing, and other assorted expenses to cover, then six months is most likely not even sufficient, and you should have enough for closer to nine months' living expenses.

If you go to **hellowallet.com/emergencysavings** you can get some help on coming up with the number that's best for you. This might seem like a daunting task but trust me, the potential downside is horrendous, and it is absolutely necessary. It's not a new concept; Aesop wrote about it in "The Ant and the Grasshopper" a couple thousand years ago. Think of it as paying into an insurance policy, only you get to keep the premiums. Remember though, this is an ***emergency fund*** and is not to be used for that shiny new car you've been dreaming about or a trip to Vegas for the Final Four.

The Retirement Fund

If you know how much money you'll need when you retire it's easy to figure out how much to save today. But you don't, so you're left with the question: Just how much money do most people need to live on in retirement? Estimates range anywhere from 70% to 95% of pre-retirement income, but the majority of financial planners suggest 80% to 85%, depending on how much you plan to travel plus health care considerations. Of course for Millennials it's a long time till retirement and you have no idea what your pre-retirement income might be, but fortunately there are some guidelines to help you.

One often cited rule of thumb says you should save 25 times the amount you expect to live on in retirement, minus whatever you get from Social Security. For example, if you think you're going to need $100,000 a year in your "golden years," and you collect $30,000 from Social Security, you'll need around $1.75 million in your 401k to provide the $70,000 difference each year. This is a good rule of thumb as you near retirement, but once again, you're too far from retirement to have a clue what you'll need in your golden years.

Guidance from Fidelity offers a different way to approach the problem. To increase your chances of having enough money in retirement Fidelity suggests that by age 35 you should have saved an amount equal to your annual salary; by age 45, three times your salary; by age 55, five times salary; and by age 65 you should have saved eight times your current salary.

A plan I like more, presented in *The Charles Schwab Guide to Finances After Fifty*, by Carrie Schwab-Pomerantz offers the following savings targets. If you're starting in your twenties you need to save 10% - 15% of your income and maintain that rate until you retire. If you wait till your thirties, you'll need to up the percentage to 15% - 25%. Put off saving till you're in your forties and it's 25% - 35%, and if you're a real procrastinator and don't get started till in your fifties, it requires saving a whopping 40% or more of your income to reach your goal. The Center for Retirement Research at Boston College

---

Suds – As the third most consumed beverage in the world, after water and tea, beer holds a place of honor for billions of folks. So I'd like to share a few random factoids with you about the golden nectar. If you suffer from cenosillicaphobia – fear of an empty glass – you might want to charge your stein before proceeding.
- In Amsterdam alcoholics are paid in beer to sweep the streets: five beers plus ten Euros.
- In 1977, Guinness world record holder Steve Petrosino downed one liter of beer in 1.3 seconds. In 2010 he chugged a 12 ounce brew in 0.18 seconds
- Snake Venom, the world's strongest beer, has a 67.5% alcohol content.
- While building the pyramids at Giza, the workers were given four liters of beer daily.
- Buddhist monks in Thailand built a temple out of 1.5 million beer bottles.
- The Babylonians would drown a brew-master in his own beer if he made a bad batch.
- Most of Oktoberfest is in September.
- When Niels Bohr won the Nobel Prize in physics in 1922, Carlsberg Brewery gave him a house next to the brewery with a direct pipeline to their tanks.
- The Vikings believed that in Valhalla (heaven) there was a giant goat named Heiorún whose utters provided an unlimited supply of beer.

Crunched some numbers and reports you would need to save 27% at age 45, while another study reports a twenty-five year old should save 16.6% of income. These are generally in line with the Schwab-Pomerantz book so I believe using her income percentage targets is the simplest and best way to go for young savers. You can then fine tune your program using salary multiples as you get closer to retirement.

Some financial advisors suggest a lifecycle approach to savings where you start out small and gradually increase your savings so that during the last ten to twenty years before retirement, you're aggressively salting away money. This escalating blueprint uses a logic similar to the government's "safe harbor" 401k plans discussed earlier, but I believe it to be a flawed logic. As we'll see, the sooner you start saving, the better.

Other Challenges

Of course an emergency fund and retirement accounts aren't the only money matters you'll need to worry about as you go through life. Besides paying for a car and saving for a down payment on a house, the cost of raising children and their education can be daunting.

According to the Department of Labor, the cost of rearing a child up to age eighteen is now around a quarter million dollars, not counting college. Wow! As expected, it's more expensive in the northeast and on the left coast than in the mid-west or south, but any way you look at it, it's big bucks.

The cost of higher education is driving more and more people to the poorhouse. The sad part of this whole education debacle is that 40 million Americans have now amassed student debt totaling $1.3 trillion, with the average individual debt around $29,000. Student loan debt has now overtaken credit card and auto loan debt, and only mortgage liabilities are a bigger financial burden.

An even more tragic effect is that for each dollar spent on student loan debt, it's one less dollar going into savings, retirement plans or used to qualify for a mortgage. Pew Research analysis showed that the median net worth of households without student debt was nearly three times greater than in households with outstanding student debt. It makes one wonder what will happen when this debt bomb finally explodes.

The Miracle of Compounding

As you can see, life is not cheap. When saving for something in the future, be it college, retirement or anything else, the sooner you start, the better. In the introduction, I said one of the four things needed to accumulate wealth is time. Time allows you to take advantage of "the miracle of compounding."

When I was a young boy, my dad and I were playing checkers, and he asked me if I would rather have $1,000 (a tidy sum back then) or a bunch of pennies on my half of the checkerboard arranged as follows: One cent on the first square, two on the next, four on the next, and so forth, doubling the number of pennies on each square till all 32 squares had coins on them. Well, the math worked out to a choice between $1,000 or more than $21 million. That rather extreme example was my introduction to compounding. While not as dramatic as the checkerboard illustration, the miracle of compounding is most noticeable for savers who start early.

Bubba and his twin sister, Bubbette, were both savers, however as a teenager, Bubba ran away from home to join the circus and became a rhinoceros trainer, and didn't start saving until he was 31 years old. He then invested $2,000 every year for the next 35 years. His sister started saving $2,000 every year once she finished college at age 22, but quit after nine years when she, too, ran off to join the circus where she became a clown.

Send the Kids Away – Besides being expensive, raising kids can be a daunting task and sometimes you might wish you could just ship them off somewhere. Well it's happened. The Post Office started parcel post service on 1 January 1913, and within two weeks someone wanted to ship a child. Mr. and Mrs. Jesse Beauge of Batavia, Ohio, "mailed" their son to his grandmother a mile away. He needed 15 cents postage and was insured for $50. A couple weeks after that Mr. and Mrs. J. W Savis of Pine Hollow, Pennsylvania, affixed 45 cents postage to their daughter and sent her to relatives. The following year, five-year-old May Pierstorff of Grangeville, Idaho, was sent to her grandparents 73 miles away, which prompted the Postmaster General to issue a memo barring the shipping of children. Not everyone got the memo however, and in 1915, six-year-old Edna Neff was sent from her mother's home in Pensacola, Florida, to her father in Christianburg, Virginia, at a cost of 15 cents.

Edna made the trip twice more that year, and other kids were mailed in Missouri and Kentucky. Over the ensuing years several more children were sent via mail until 1920, when the practice was officially forbidden. In case you were wondering, all the children were under the 50 pound Parcel Post weight limit.

In total, Bubbette put in $18,000 while her brother contributed $70,000. They each invested their money in a mutual fund with a 9% annual rate of return. So, who ended up with the bigger stash when they retired from the circus? Look at the bottom line to see the value of their accounts. The take-away here is not that clowns are smarter than rhino trainers, but that you can accumulate more, even if you invest less, when you start early.

It's easy to see that the secret is to become a super-saver and stash away as much as you can as early as you can. Don't delay. A small amount of money saved in your twenties and thirties grows into a much bigger nest egg than a larger amount saved by the procrastinator in his 40s. End of story!

A Double-Edged Sword

Like a United States Marine, compounding can be your best friend or worst enemy. The miracle of compounding also has its yin and yang, its light and dark, its good and bad. The dark side of compounding is called inflation. Just as compounding allows your savings to grow, it likewise allows inflation to take an ever increasing toll on the value of your money.

For example, with a 3½% inflation rate, a $60,000 full-sized pickup truck will cost $62,100 after one year, $84,000 in only ten years, $119,000 in 20 years and an astounding $168,000 in 30 years. Inflation, like time, waits for no one. (Can you imagine paying $168,000 for a pickup?) To get out in front of the eroding effects of inflation you have to start saving early. If you're not saving, inflation is eating your lunch.

Age	Bubba	Bubbette
22		$2,000.00
23		$2,000.00
24		$2,000.00
25		$2,000.00
26		$2,000.00
27		$2,000.00
28		$2,000.00
29		$2,000.00
30		$2,000.00
31	$2,000.00	
32	$2,000.00	
33	$2,000.00	
34	$2,000.00	
35	$2,000.00	
36	$2,000.00	
37	$2,000.00	
38	$2,000.00	
39	$2,000.00	
40	$2,000.00	
41	$2,000.00	
42	$2,000.00	
43	$2,000.00	
44	$2,000.00	
45	$2,000.00	
46	$2,000.00	
47	$2,000.00	
48	$2,000.00	
49	$2,000.00	
50	$2,000.00	
51	$2,000.00	
52	$2,000.00	
53	$2,000.00	
54	$2,000.00	
55	$2,000.00	
56	$2,000.00	
57	$2,000.00	
58	$2,000.00	
59	$2,000.00	
60	$2,000.00	
61	$2,000.00	
62	$2,000.00	
63	$2,000.00	
64	$2,000.00	
65	$2,000.00	
Total Invested	$70,000.00	$18,000.00
Balance Age 65	$470,249.00	$579,471.00

Cost of a $60,000 truck

#	Price	#	Price	#	Price
1	$62,100	11	$87,598	21	$123,566
2	$64,274	12	$90,664	22	$127,891
3	$66,523	13	$93,837	23	$132,367
4	$68,851	14	$97,122	24	$137,000
5	$71,261	15	$100,521	25	$141,795
6	$73,755	16	$104,039	26	$146,758
7	$76,337	17	$107,681	27	$151,894
8	$79,009	18	$111,449	28	$157,210
9	$81,774	19	$115,350	29	$162,713
10	$84,636	20	$119,387	30	$168,408

Looking back provides another perspective. Over the last 50 years, inflation in the U.S. has averaged 3.2%, which isn't all that bad, however even at that modest rate, prices double every 20 years. To give you an idea of how inflation, even low inflation, compounds over time and erodes the purchasing power of money, take a look at the chart below to see what some common things cost 25 and 50 years ago.

Starting early and letting the "miracle of compounding" work for you provides security and independence, and even better health. One study showed a strong correlation between retirement contributions and improved health. Hopefully all this has convinced you that it's in your best long term interest to start saving early.

	1965	1990	2015
Minimum wage	$1.25	$3.80	$7.15
Median household income	$6,100.00	$29,000.00	$53,000.00
Average price of a house	$21,500.00	$123,000.00	$176,700.00
First class stamp	$0.05	$0.25	$0.49
Gallon of gas	$0.31	$1.34	$2.89
Movie ticket	$1.00	$4.23	$8.12
One dozen eggs	$0.53	$1.78	$2.00
Gallon of milk	$0.95	$2.78	$3.85

Hyperinflation – When inflation exceeds 50% per month, economists call it *hyperinflation*. Could you imagine something that cost $100 this month being $150 the next month and $225 the following month? In April 1989, monthly inflation in Ecuador peaked at 99%. The only good news was that bank robberies ceased because the thieves couldn't carry enough money to make it worthwhile. That's bad, but it pales in comparison to some of the worst cases.

Inflation in the Weimar Republic (Germany) after WWI reached 29,500% per month. That means prices doubled every 3.7 days. But wait, it gets worse! In Zimbabwe in 2008, it hit 98% per day so prices doubled every day, and the government eventually was printing 100 trillion dollar bills. But the granddaddy of all inflation was in Hungary in July of 1946, with a daily rate of 207% which caused prices to double every 15 hours. Crazy!

The Bottom Line

What have we learned so far?

-- As a nation, we Americans are poor savers with poor financial literacy.

-- Over the years government policies have discouraged savings and encouraged consumption.

-- Traditional pension plans have given way to "Defined Contribution Plans," and the decision-making risk has shifted to employees.

-- Frugalers are by nature apt to save and Spendthrifts are not. You need to figure which way you lean to keep from becoming your own worst enemy.

-- "Pay yourself first" should be everyone's mantra.

-- Prepare a written budget and follow it every month.

-- Establish an emergency fund of three to six months' living expenses.

-- Start saving early for long term goals like retirement and college.

-- Compounding can be your best friend or worst enemy. Use it to your advantage.

-- Discipline is the hardest part when it comes to saving money.

Part II

Investing

"The inherent vice of capitalism is the unequal sharing of blessings.
The inherent virtue of socialism is the equal sharing of miseries."
Winston Churchill

"A rising tide lifts all boats."
John F. Kennedy

"Don't confuse genius with a bull market."
J. Kenneth Galbraith

"I can calculate the movement of stars, but not the madness of men".
Issac Newton, scientist and investor

"Risk comes from not knowing what you're doing."
Warren Buffett

"There is only one thing about investing that I am absolutely sure of: The lower the expense that I pay to the purveyor of an investment service, the more money there will be for me.
Burton Malkiel, Author (*A Random Walk Down Wall Street*)

Bulls make money, bears make money, and pigs get slaughtered.
Old Wall Street saying

"Time is your friend; impulse is your enemy."
Jack Bogle, founder, Vanguard Group

"Beer is proof that God loves us and wants us to be happy."
Benjamin Franklin

The Big Picture

Since the risk shift in pension plans put the decision making onus on workers, some understanding of stocks and bonds and how the markets work is necessary to maximize your investments. When you invest in stocks and bonds, you're not just purchasing shares in some company; you're investing in an economic system. Capitalism is an economic system based on the creation of goods and services for profit, and has served humankind well. Many people scoff at the word "profit," but over the years, capitalism has lifted hundreds of millions of people out of subsistence poverty around the world. Combine capitalism with a freely elected government, a free press, property rights, and the rule of law, and you have a very powerful engine providing opportunity for people to pursue their dreams and achieve greatness.

In the following pages we're going to cover stocks, bonds and other investments. We'll get into some history and theory (just a little) so you can better understand the "why" of what's involved and we'll look at strategies to reduce risk, which hopefully will make you feel more confident in creating a portfolio that you won't loose sleep over. Depending on how much you're into it, investing can be as simple or complex as you want to make it so I'm going to give you four options from easy peasy to more advanced.

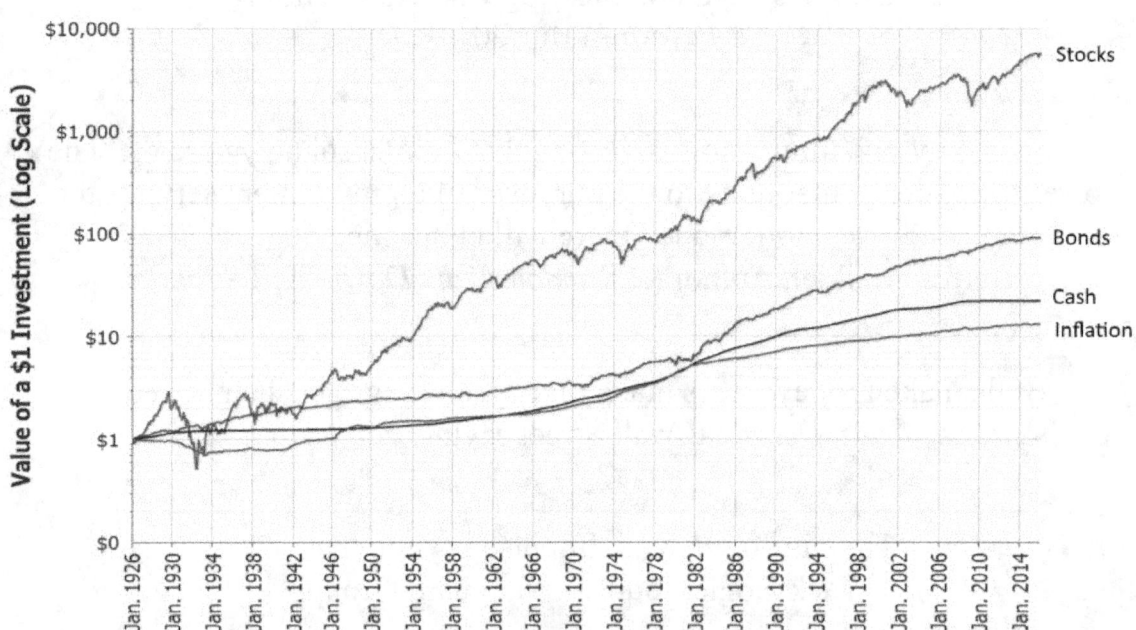

Source: ChartSource®, Wealth Management Systems Inc. For the period from January 1, 1926, through December 31, 2015. Stocks are represented by the S&P 500 index. Bonds are represented by a composite of the total returns of long-term U.S. government bonds, derived from yields published by the Federal Reserve through 1972, the Barclays Long-Term Government Bond index through 1975, and the Barclays U.S. Aggregate index thereafter. Cash is represented by a composite of the yields of 3-month Treasury bills, published by the Federal Reserve, and the Barclays 3-Month Treasury Bills index. Inflation is represented by the change in the Consumer Price Index. It is not possible to invest directly in an index. Past performance is not a guarantee of future results. Copyright © 2016, Wealth Management Systems Inc. All rights reserved. Not responsible for any errors or omissions.

If you're one of those people that's just not into financial planning and Part I made your eyes glaze over, I'm afraid you may need a little more root-beer or grape juice to get through some parts of this chapter. There's no way to sugar coat it. This is going to be tough, but you made it this far and it's a short book. It's not like you're reading *War and Peace.* Just remember, those who like this stuff the least are usually the ones who need it the most, so hang in there. I promise (cross my heart) there's a simple investing strategy that's custom made for you and it's not too many pages away. By the end of this chapter you'll be better prepared for the investment decisions you're going to have to make. Trust me, it's a winner, winner, chicken dinner. Let's get started.

Creative Destruction

Capitalism is by no means perfect but it is the best thing we've come up with thus far in human history. In earlier times barter worked to a certain extent but is ill suited for today's complex, globalized society. Communism had a go of it for a good part of the last century but didn't provide incentive for workers and failed to lift the standard of living for the masses. Capitalism is a much better system, but capitalism unchecked is not a good thing. The role of government in a capitalistic society is to provide enough regulation and control to prevent greed from running amok, yet not so much that it stifles creativity and entrepreneurship. Balancing these is an unending battle between the left and the right sides of the political spectrum.

Capitalism is certainly not without risk. As a matter of fact, risk is a very basic part of the system. Capitalism provides the freedom for an entrepreneur to start a company but also the freedom to fail. One third of new businesses fail in the first two years, and more than half fail in the first four years. Yet the opportunity to create something and succeed has been a siren song to millions around the world seeking to better themselves.

This risk is not limited to new businesses either. There's risk for large established companies in a capitalistic system. In what economists call "creative destruction," entire industries have failed and fallen by the wayside. Consider that little more than a century ago, huge numbers of workers were employed around a transportation industry based on the horse and buggy. The arrival of the automobile changed things almost overnight as blacksmiths, buggy makers, wheelwrights, and thousands who shoveled manure from city streets, (Ah! What a job.) watched their livelihood disappear within a couple of decades.

Creative destruction continues to this day. Twenty-five years ago the Internet and cell phones were in their infancy, but now they're a ubiquitous part of our culture, impacting libraries, publishing, and wire-line communications. Much to my personal consternation print newspapers, magazines and books are going the way of the horse and buggy. For all the angst creative destruction produced in the horse and buggy era, even greater numbers of jobs were created in the auto industry that replaced it, and today are being created as part of the internet revolution. How many other industries can you think of which have fallen to new technologies?

- With the advent of digital photography, do you see film in stores anymore? Of course not. It went to the scrap heap with typewriters, vinyl records and cassette tapes.

- Have you noticed that foot traffic at the mall has been declining, and there are more and more empty storefronts, as brick and mortar retailers close due to on-line shopping. What will become of these malls? How about apartment complexes, office parks or schools - Ye Olde Towne Centre Mall University.

- Banks used to brag about how many branch offices they had but now, because of on-line banking, are closing them in droves. Some banks now even charge a fee for face time with a living, breathing teller.

- In New York City, taxis must have a city-issued license known as a medallion, because it is literally a medal medallion bolted to the hood of the cab. Medallions are

> **Luddites** – Creative destruction rarely takes place without disruption. When the Industrial Revolution threatened the livelihood of English textile workers in the early nineteenth century, bands of workers, mostly self-employed weavers, began destroying the power looms that they saw as threatening their jobs. They called themselves Luddites after Ned Ludd, who smashed some stocking frames in a fit of rage in a mill in 1779. After they assassinated a mill owner, the British Army stepped in and arrested more than 60 Luddites. In January 1813 the government put on a massive show trial to discourage further insurrection. Some Luddites were hanged and others sent to penal colonies, and the movement soon faded. The term Luddite eventually came to refer to anyone opposed to new technology.

expensive, and in 2014 cost just over $1 million. Along came Uber and the price of a medallion quickly fell about 40%. Many drivers took out short-term loans to finance their medallions and now with prices falling are unable to refinance.

Creative destruction can be painful. Of the original companies in the Dow Jones Industrial Average created in 1896, which were marquis corporations of their day, only General Electric remains. American Cotton Oil, National Lead and U.S. Leather have given way to the likes of Apple, Hewlett-Packard, Home Depot, Intel, IBM, Wal-Mart and Disney.

There can be personal as well as investment consequences to creative destruction that I'm sometimes not happy about. We now have driver-less cars and pilot-less aircraft, and computer generated graphics are becoming so advanced that the day will come when you won't be able to tell the difference between an avatar and a real person. Imagine your favorite actors being replaced in films and on television by computer generated images. Live theater might be the last remaining venue for human performers, and Oscar night might reward the human creative genius of writers, costume designers, and computer geeks, but not actors.

Recently someone passed the famous Turing Test, when a computer convinced enough

---

An Imitation Game – In 1950, noted British computing scientist Alan Turing posed his famous question: "Can machines think?" A popular parlor game in the Victorian era was called the Imitation Game and involved two people, a man and a woman, trying to convince the rest of the guests that each is the woman. They would go to separate rooms and answer written questions. The written answers were read by a neutral referee. The woman had to tell the truth while the man did not as he attempted to convince the guests he was the woman.

Inspired by this game, Turing proposed a similar test to see if people could detect if they were communicating with a human or a machine, and predicted that by the year 2000 a machine would indeed fool a human.

The structure of the test in recent years, has a person and a computer placed in separate rooms, with several judges in a third room. Each judge is allowed five minutes of real-time, simultaneous, text-based conversations to try and determine which subject is not human. No preset topics or questions are required in the text conversations and 30 percent of the judges need to be convinced for the computer to claim victory. For the first time ever, on 7 June 2014—ironically the 60th anniversary of Turing's death—a computer named "Eugene Goostman" convinced 10 of 30 judges that it was a 13 year old, non-native-English-speaking boy from Ukraine. I'm sure Turing was smiling.

judges that it was human. At least I thought, a geek won't be able to replace my favorite recording artists. Then I listened to the commencement speaker at Andrew's college graduation. Dr. Gil Weinberg, an MIT educated robotics engineer and founder of the Center for Music Technology at Georgia Tech, discussed his robot marimba player which can improvise like a jazz master. "How long 'til the robots conquer the world of music?" I thought. It pains me to even contemplate a world without the next Andrea Bocelli, Willy Nelson or the Beatles, and I'm sure you Millennials wouldn't be too excited to go see a hologram instead of the real life Rihanna, Bruno Mars, Alicia Keys, or Taylor Swift.

Moola

It's always a good idea to have some cash on hand. As a stand-alone investment, cash is often a money-losing proposition because it doesn't earn very much interest, but keeping a little cash around can allow you to take advantage of investment opportunities. Though some might want to keep their cash under the mattress or buried in a Mason jar in the back yard, it's safer to keep it in a bank or credit union or as part of an investment account. Interestingly, since 1926, cash has outperformed stocks about one-third of the time and outperformed bonds about one-third of the time, but has only beaten both stocks and bonds 12% of the time. More on that later.

When markets take a dive, be it the stock market, real-estate market, or any other market, cash is king. People who don't maintain some cash on hand could end up in what's called an asset-rich, cash-poor position. I once spoke with a woman whose husband had lost his job. Work was hard to find and they were in danger of falling behind with their mortgage payments. They were both in their 50's and had all their assets tied up in their home, with

---

Why 1926? – If you look at charts showing the performance of the stock market you might notice that they often start in 1926. Legend says that in 1959, someone at Merrill Lynch came upon boxes of old records going back to December 1925. Merrill then asked the University of Chicago's Booth School of Business to analyze them and compute rates of return for stocks relative to other assets. With a grant from Merrill Lynch, the Center for Research in Security Prices (CRSP) was created in 1960, to compile and analyze a long-term database. The massive undertaking was completed in 1964, and has been added to ever since.

Another version of the story is that researchers at CRSP randomly chose 1926, so as to include at least one full business cycle prior to the Great Depression. I prefer the dusty-boxes-in-the-basement scenario, but whatever the reason, most data regarding long-term returns for stocks and other assets begin with 1926.

no emergency fund. This was their dream home that they wanted to live in forever. Even though they had several hundred thousand dollars equity in their home, they couldn't qualify for a home equity line of credit or cash-out refinancing because neither of them had a job. They were close to having to sell their dream home in a terrible down market or face being foreclosed on.

Stocks

Let's say Joe and his wife Teddy give up their careers as field hockey stars to settle down and open a small widget factory. Business is good and they want to expand, but they used all their savings to initially build the factory. One way they could raise money is to take their privately owned company public, by selling shares of stock (also referred to as equities) in their widget factory. Each share of stock would represent a fractional ownership in The Widget Company.

There are two main forms of stock but the most common is, well, *common stock*. It's the stock that they're talking about on the six o'clock news when they give the market update for the day. There is also *preferred stock* which is higher in the pecking order when it comes to dividends and settling claims if a company were to go out of business. Stocks are

---

Bull & Bear – Where did the terms Bull and Bear come from? No one knows for sure but the two most common stories each have some credibility. In early California, promoters would put on fights between a bull and a bear and charge a dollar a head to witness the blood sport. The upward thrust of the bull's horns and the downward swing from the bear's claws came to represent the upward and downward movements of the market. (Unfortunately for the bulls, which were in plentiful supply, the fights were often rigged in favor of the rarer and more expensive bears, by sawing off the bull's horns or constraining them with ropes.)

Another story says that middlemen in the fur trade would often sell bearskins before they got them from the trappers, speculating on that year's supply and hoping to make a greater profit from the spread between the price they paid and their selling price. When there was an abundance of skins, these bearskin jobbers or "bears," paid less for each skin, so among the trappers a falling price for their goods became known as a "bear" market. Since bears and bulls were considered enemies, in the sporting arena at least, the term "bull" acquired an opposite meaning.

also categorized by the type and size of the corporation into what is called a Morningstar StyleBox™, created by the Morningstar Corporation. Here's an example of a style box for a Large Cap growth company.

The size of a company is determined by market capitalization, referred to as market cap. Market cap is the number of outstanding shares multiplied by its share price. For example, if the Widget Company had one million shares outstanding and they were selling at $10 a share, the market cap would be $10 million. There are no official definitions for large, medium and small cap companies, but generally speaking small cap is around $300 million to $2 billion, medium cap is $2 billion to $10 billion, and large cap is greater than $10 billion. Usually, the smaller the corporation, the greater the volatility and risk when you're investing.

Equity Style Box

	Value	Blend	Growth
Large			■
Medium			
Small			

Morningstar StyleBox™ Chart

Source: © 2016 Morningstar, Inc. All Rights Reserved. Reproduced with permission. *

As you can see, the types of stock in the style box are value, growth, or blend. Value stocks typically pay higher dividends than the market average and are slightly less volatile. Growth stock companies are expected to grow at an above average rate because they put most of their earnings back into the company rather than pay a dividend. Investors in growth stocks expect to make a profit primarily through price appreciation while value investors are happy to collect steady dividends with maybe a little price appreciation. A blend is just what it says, stocks with aspects of both growth and value.

Bonds

Another way Joe and Teddy could raise money for expanding The Widget Company is by selling bonds. Unlike stocks, where the investor is purchasing a piece of the company, a bond purchaser is making a loan to the company, usually in return for a fixed interest rate for a specific period of time, so bonds are referred to as fixed-income securities. For example, a ten year 5% bond for $10,000 would pay $500 interest per year for ten years at which time the bondholders would receive their $10,000 principle. There is also a Morningstar StyleBox™ for bonds based on the term of the bond and its credit quality.
In this example, the highlighted area tells you it's a long-term, medium-grade bond or bond fund. Like the capitalization of a company in the stock style box, the term of a bond is somewhat subjective as to whether it is short or medium. Generally speaking, short-term

The Buttonwood Tree – In 1790, treasury secretary Alexander Hamilton issued $80 million worth of bonds to help pay for the Revolutionary War. Financial transactions for these bonds usually took place in offices, coffeehouses, and auction houses. To bring order to this disjointed system of security trading for government bonds and other securities, a couple dozen brokers met on 17 May 1792, at their usual meeting place under a buttonwood tree at 86 Wall Street and drafted an agreement to form the New York Stock & Exchange Board. This early agreement stated that they would only deal with each other and the commission would be set at 0.25%.

Within a year there were too many brokers to meet under the tree so they moved to the Tontine Coffee House at the corner of Wall Street and Water Street, but if weather allowed, they conducted their business outdoors. In 1863 a more formal constitution was drafted, and the name was officially shortened to the New York Stock Exchange. In 1868, the exchange established a fixed number of memberships, or "seats" that sold for around $4,000. In 2005 a NYSE seat sold for a record $4 million.

bonds are from one to three years, medium-term bonds are from three to ten years, and long-term bonds are more than ten years.

U.S. government fixed-income securities are referred to as bills, notes, or bonds. Treasury bills (or T-bills) mature in one year or less, while treasury notes are for two, three, five, seven and ten years, and treasury bonds are more than ten years.

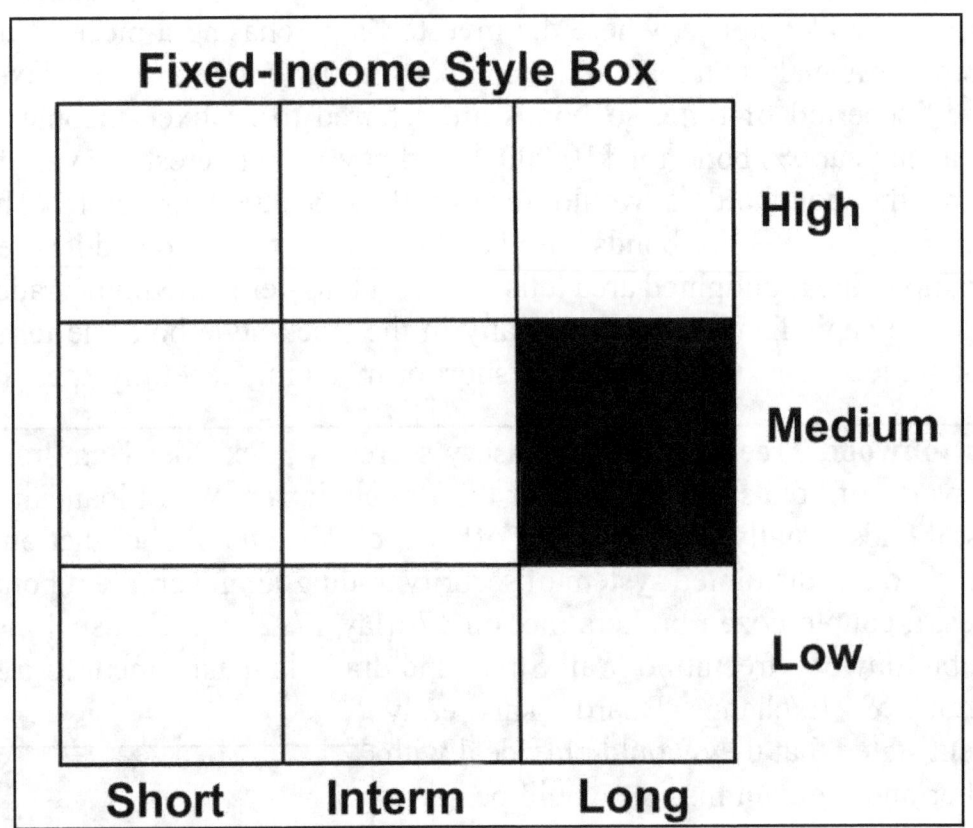

Morningstar StyleBox™ Chart

Source: © 2016 Morningstar, Inc. All Rights Reserved. Reproduced with permission. *

Though bonds are generally considered safer than stocks, they are not without risk. The credit worthiness of a fixed-income investment is usually determined by one or more of three major credit rating agencies (CRA). Standard and Poor's, Moody's, and Fitch have each been in the business of rating the credit worthiness of businesses for more than 100 years and control 95% of the CRA market in the U.S. The Big Three, as they are known, use slightly different formats when issuing ratings for bonds. The following chart will give you an idea of what the ratings look like.

Moody's	Standard & Poor's	Fitch	
Aaa		AAA	Prime
Aa1	AAA	AA+	
Aa2	AA+	AA	High Quality
Aa3	AA	AA-	
A1	AA-	A+	
A2	A+	A	Upper Medium
A3	A	A-	Grade
Baa1	A-	BBB+	
Baa2	BBB+	BBB	
Baa3	BBB	BBB-	Lower Medium
Ba1	BBB-	BB+	Grade
Ba2	BB+	BB	
Ba3	BB	BB-	Non-Investment
B1	BB-	B+	Grade
B2	B+	B	
B3	B	B-	
Caa1	B-		
Caa2	CCC+		Speculative
Caa3	CCC	CCC	
	CCC-		Substantial Risk
Ca	CC		Extremely
	C		Speculative

The ratings actually go on into the D's but you can get the gist of how it works from the chart. Here's all you need to remember about bond ratings. Bonds rated BBB- and above (Baa3 for Moody's) are considered investment grade. Lower rated non-investment grade securities are often referred to as "junk" bonds. Double B "junk" has a very low default rate and isn't so bad but going too far below BB gets risky. Obviously, the lower the credit rating of the company issuing the bond, the higher the interest rate required to compensate investors for the increased risk of default. This is is known as credit risk.

Bond prices and interest rates have what's called an inverse relationship. When interest rates rise, bond prices fall and when rates fall, prices rise. This might sound bass-ackwards and fog your brain, so let's take a moment to look at why this happens. Suppose you had a ten year $1,000 bond with a 5% interest rate that you wanted to sell. And suppose that there is a buyer who is looking for a ten year $1,000 bond, but that interest rates have now fallen to 4%. If the buyer wants to purchase your 5% bond, he or she will have to pay a premium and you might get $1,075 for your $1,000 bond. On the other hand, if rates have risen to say 6%, you would have to discount your 5% bond and might only get $925 for it, because no one in their right mind would pay full price for a bond paying 5% when 6% bonds are readily available. This is referred to as interest rate risk or market risk.

I once spoke with a man who had $1 million in retirement savings and wanted to be very conservative, so he split it between two different brokers, and then put the entire amount in highly rated municipal bonds. This, of course was against the advice of both brokers, but he thought it was the safest course of action. When interest rates went up, he got an introduction to interest rate risk, and was much dismayed to find his portfolio was no longer worth $1 million.

Longer term bonds have more interest rate risk so higher interest rates are usually required. If you owned a two year bond and rates rose, you could hang on to for two years and cash out, but what if it were a 30 year bond? Holding on till it matured might not be an option, so longer bonds need to provide higher interest rates to compensate investors for the added risk. This is called duration risk.

Bottoms up – There are more than 10,000 craft breweries in the world with around 4,000 in the US, 4,000 in Europe, and the rest scattered across the globe. That means there are umpteen thousand different beers to enjoy as you roam the planet. But just about all these brews fall into just two categories: ales and lagers. The difference is in the yeasts used in the brewing process, and though both are beers, the final products are as different as red and white wines.

In the fermentation tanks, ale yeasts ferment at the top and thrive at a warmer temperature of around 60 to 72 degrees F. After fermentation, ales are usually aged a couple weeks at 40 to 55 degrees F and come out of the tanks with rich, soft, warm and complex flavors. They're best served cool or near room temperature. Examples of ales are Pale Ale, IPA, Porter and Stout.

The more aggressive lager yeasts do better at cooler temperatures (46 to 55 degrees F) and ferment near the bottom of the tank. They typically are then aged for several months at near-freezing temperatures (32 to 45 degrees F). This aging is called lagering and yields a drier, cleaner, crisper beer. Lagers are the most popular beers and are best served cold. They can be light such as Pilsner, and Helles or dark like Bock, Oktoberfest and Dunkle.

Though there are only two categories of beer, there are many styles based on the ingredients used and how they're prepared, so you can have light ales and dark lagers and a wide range of flavors.

Some other common risks are:
Inflation Risk – If you have a 4% bond and inflation goes to 5%, you're losing money.
Currency Risk – Foreign bonds are often in the currency of the country of the issuer, and if the dollar strengthens against that currency you get fewer dollars.
Call Risk – Callable bonds allow the issuer to purchase the bond back at their discretion, which they often do when interest rates fall.

Time Horizon

How much of your assets you should put in stocks, bonds, cash and other investments is called asset allocation, and we'll cover it in more detail later, but you should know that there are situations, based on your time horizon, where you might want to be totally invested in stocks and other times when you would not want to be in stocks at all. It all depends on your time horizon. If you're saving for a near-term goal, say buying a car or down payment on a house two or three years in the future, it would be foolish to have that money in the stock market. Put it in the credit union, or bank, but not in the stock market. There's just too much risk, considering that the worst one year return in the U.S. stock market was a loss of almost 50%. (The best one year return was a gain of more than 60%.) That's way too much volatility for a short term goal.

However, the good news is that if you're investing for long term goals such as retirement, a child's education, or anything 15, 20, or even 30 years in the future, stock market risk decreases as time periods lengthen. Think about this: Stocks have produced a positive return 95% of the time in rolling 10 year periods. For example, the worst 10 year return in market history was only -1.3% annually from 1928 to 1937 (the best 10 year period was 19.5% annually from 1918 to 1927). When we look out longer term, the news is even better. There has never been a 20 year period where the stock market has lost money, the worst period being from 1928 to 1947, when the yearly gain averaged 2.5%. So the bottom line is this: When you're investing for the long term, you need to have a good chunk of your money invested in the stock market because stocks provide the best foundation for long term success.

Barry Pencek
Trading vs. Investing

In a nutshell, the difference between trading and investing is time. Investing is longer-term, usually months or years, while trading is short-term, sometimes only days or hours. Investors, through analysis and research, buy stocks they think have good growth potential and hope to make a profit over time through price appreciation. Or they build a portfolio of stocks that pay nice dividends to augment income or accumulate additional shares by reinvesting the dividends. They are in for the longer haul and not concerned with short-term fluctuations in price. Slow and steady wins the day for investors.

Traders, on the other hand, are much more active with a much shorter outlook, and thrive on volatility. Using charts and technical analysis they buy and sell quickly to take profits or cut losses. So-called day traders buy a stock or short a stock (more on that later), hoping to get out at the end of the day and turn a profit. Others, called scalpers do basically the same type of trades dozens of times a day and may hold a position for only minutes.

Studies have shown that most traders under-perform the S&P500 (an index of large cap stocks) long term and up to 80% lose money in the first year. Additionally, if a trader does make a profit, he or she will pay higher taxes because it's a short term gain. The worst thing that could happen to anyone who starts trading is to luck out and hit it big early on, because it would set the hook and they'd be addicted, like many Las Vegas gamblers who win big on their first outing. However if you're a high-adrenalin, high-stress type person who likes excitement, and absolutely must try your hand at trading, there are a few guidelines you should remember: Use only money you can afford to lose, commit no more than 10 percent of your portfolio, never use leverage, and stay away from penny stocks (those trading for less than one dollar). Though I'd personally recommend a trip to Vegas where you can get free drinks while you gamble, some people just have it in their DNA to take the plunge.

On the positive side, traders are better at selling a falling stock because they always have an escape plan to sell at a predetermined price. Investors on the other hand often develop an emotional attachment to a stock and are reluctant to dump a loser.

Famed investor Warren Buffett learned at an early age the value of holding onto a sound investment. In his early years Buffett bought shares in a company for $38 and they quickly dropped to $27. It scared him but he held on and the stock recovered. He sold at $40 and made a small profit. Young Warren was 11 years old at the time. He came to regret that decision as he watched the shares go to $200 and later claimed that is what taught him the importance of being a patient investor.

Market Timing

Old Farts Rule – In Asia, old people are revered for their knowledge and wisdom. Not so much in the United States these days, so when people in their 80's and 90's are sought for their opinions, they must have something to say that's worth listening to. Here are a few investing old timers who have been around the block once or twice and have withstood the test of time.

Benjamin Graham – Born in Britain in 1894, Graham is considered the father of value Investing and according to Warren Buffett, his 1949 book "The Intelligent Investor" is "by far the best book on investing ever written." Graham died in 1976 but his book is still widely read.

Warren Buffett – The "Oracle of Omaha" was born in 1930 with investing in his blood. On a family trip to New York at age ten, young Warren wanted to see the New York Stock Exchange. At age 11 he purchased six shares of Cities Services (three for him and three for his sisters), and filed his first tax return at age 14, where he took a $35 deduction for use of his bicycle on his paper route. In high school he bought a farm. A math prodigy, he started college at the University of Pennsylvania at age 16, but finished at the University of Nebraska with a B.S. in business at age 19. Buffet then went to Columbia Business School so he could study economics under Benjamin Graham, the person he credits with influencing him the most throughout his life.

Jack Bogle – The "father of index investing" was born in New Jersey in 1929. While at Princeton in 1951, Bogle posited that since three out of four mutual funds did not beat their benchmark, one could get a better return and lower fees, by investing in the index itself. In 1974 he founded the Vanguard Group, putting his index philosophy to the test when he created the first retail S&P 500 Index Fund. Today Vanguard has $2 trillion in assets. Bogle was heavily influenced by the writings of Burton Malkiel.

Burton Malkiel – This noted Ivy League professor was born in 1932 and a proponent of the "efficient market hypothesis." Malkiel is most famous to laymen for his book *A Random Walk Down Wall Street*. He served on the board of the Vanguard Group with his friend John Bogle for 28 years, before retiring in 2005.

It seems like a simple enough concept: Buy low, sell high. Over time, stocks (including dividends) will earn about a 10% annual return. But, if you could just buy them when the market is at its lowest point and sell them at the top, you would make a killing. If you had invested $10,000 in an index of the 500 largest companies in the U.S. in 2001, and sold ten years later, your investment would have grown to about $11,500. Not a great return. However, if you sold at the beginning of the down years and bought the index again at the beginning of the up years, you would have gotten more than $26,000.

The only problem is knowing when to act. Human nature causes many people to panic and sell after a stock has fallen, and then buy again long after the price has risen, in effect buying high and selling low, the exact opposite of what was intended.

Perhaps market timing is not impossible, but it's a very difficult thing to do because it requires two correct calls: when to get out and when to get back in. Independent tracking of market timers over several decades shows they do no better than chance, because that's exactly what market timing is: a game of chance.

A Couple of Smart Guys

Brace yourself, we're about to get into the basics of building a portfolio. This may require some liquid courage to get through, but hang in there because it'll help you understand the "why" of portfolio construction. (Boy, does that sound boring!) Oh well, let's get started.

Harry Markowitz was born in Chicago in 1927. He was a math whiz and got his PhD at the University of Chicago where he used mathematical analysis of the stock market to study the effects of diversification on portfolio performance. He wrote a paper in 1952 called *Portfolio Selection,* and it was the genesis for what became known as Modern Portfolio Theory (MPT). Later he went to work for the Rand Corporation outside Los Angeles.

About the same time, another smart guy named William Sharpe pursued a PhD at UCLA and was in search of a dissertation topic. In 1956 he also took a job at Rand where he met Markowitz and decided to build on his portfolio theory. Sharp further established the relationship between stock selection and risk/reward. Their body of work shattered many sacred Wall Street ideas of the time and in 1990,

Markowitz and Sharpe were awarded the Nobel Memorial Prize in Economic Science.
In a nutshell, MPT attempts to maximize return and minimize risk through portfolio construction. It approaches investing by looking at the market as a whole and shows that having the proper allocation of stocks, bonds and cash is more important than the performance of individual assets within the portfolio. A balanced portfolio allows you to capture most of the gains of the market while minimizing the downside risk. This happens because different asset groups move in different directions. For example the stock market and bond market don't always move up or down at the same time, nor do large cap stocks and small cap stocks, or commodities and stocks.

Basically, Markowitz and Sharpe are a couple of really smart hombres who spent years to come up with some very complex mathematical formulas to prove what grandma always told you: don't put all your eggs in one basket.

It didn't take long for other researchers to try and figure out just how much portfolio construction actually contributed to performance. In 1986, three economists named Brinson, Hood and Beebower published a paper, known as the BHB Study, stating that 91% of portfolio return was due to asset allocation, 5% due to selection (individual stocks or bonds), and 4% to timing. This was kind of earth-shattering news and touched off the "90% debate" with researchers everywhere coming up with answers ranging from 40%, to 75% to 100%.

> **Broken Eggs** – I once flew a trip with a Captain who was reading several books on investment real estate. (Not while flying.) He explained that he had 18 months until retirement and wanted to build a portfolio of income properties to generate cash when he stopped flying.
>
> A couple years earlier, United Airlines had an Employee Stock Ownership Program (ESOP) which allowed employees to buy shares in the company and he had a considerable number of shares. They also had a defined benefit plan and a 401(k). Since his 401(k) was self directed, he had put all of the money into United stock. He said he understood the airline business and thought United had a bright future. When the airline filed for bankruptcy, he lost just about everything. The ESOP shares were near valueless. The defined benefit plan was taken over by the government and he was to receive about 35% of what would have been his traditional pension and since he put his entire 401(k) into UAL stock, it was pretty much worthless too. He had put all of his eggs in the UAL basket, the basket had fallen, and the eggs were shattered along with his retirement dreams. I never saw the guy again and have often wondered how he made out in retirement. If only he'd known just a little about asset allocation and diversification.

If you ever have insomnia and need a sleep aid, just start reading any of these studies and you'll be lights out in no time. I'm not knocking their profession, and my hat's off to anyone who does economic or financial research, but it's just not my cup of tea. The take away here however, is to realize that asset allocation is a very, very important, if not the most important, determinant of portfolio performance.

To show you how powerful MPT based investing can be let me tell you about one study I looked at. (Must have had insomnia.) It compared three different, one million dollar portfolios, one invested in bonds, one invested in stocks, and one a mixture of 60% stocks and 40% bonds. They each had annual withdrawals starting at $60,000 and increasing by 3.5% every year to account for inflation. It covered a 38 year period, from 1970 to 2007 using real world numbers. As expected the stock portfolio had the highest average annual return, but the results at the end were not what you might expect. The all bond portfolio went broke in 2003 after 34 years. The all stock portfolio, even though it had the highest annual return, was at zero in 2007 while the 60/40 balanced portfolio had a balance of $1.3 million. Holy schmoley, that's more than it started with! Even though the stock portfolio had negative returns in only eight of the 38 years, it lost so much more than the other two in those down years, that future gains couldn't make up the lost ground.

Within the general categories of stocks, bonds and cash you also need what's referred to as diversification. Let's say you built a portfolio of 60% stocks, 35% bonds and 5% cash. If however, the stock portion was entirely made up of shares in Joe and Teddy's Widget Company, you would be in a very risky position. Because the Widget Company is a small company, you should add some large and medium sized company stocks and perhaps some international companies, too. Likewise, in the bond portion you would want to spread the risk among short term and long term bonds of various credit qualities. There are also alternative asset classes that might be considered such as real estate and commodities. One good rule of thumb to prevent risk due to lack of diversification is to never put more than 5% of your assets in any one stock or industry.

Investing professionals break the market down further into ten sectors when diversifying and usually set sector weightings for each. Each sector can have its own characteristics and risk profile, and there may be several industries within each. The Widget Company, for example, would fit into the Industrial sector. Here they are:

Consumer Discretionary	**Industrials**
Consumer Staples	**Information Technology**
Energy	**Materials**
Financials	**Telecommunication Services**
Health Care	**Utilities**

We're Only Human

It wasn't too long before criticism of MPT began to build. Some complained that the model neglected alternate investments, taxes and fees, but the biggest criticism was that MPT didn't reflect the real world, and that Markowitz and Sharpe crunched numbers but ignored the behavior of the people behind the numbers. Perhaps they assumed investors were rational and logical human beings when in fact we are anything but rational.

Emotions are involved big time, and for most of us, emotion trumps logic. It's long been said that markets run on fear and greed, but this had never been quantified. Daniel Kahneman was awarded the 2002 Nobel Prize in Economics for a 1979 paper entitled *Prospect Theory: An Analysis of Decision Under Risk* that he wrote with fellow psychologist Amos Tversky. They showed that investors tend to make irrational financial choices based on how they evaluate gains and losses. Their paper set the investment world aflutter (Did I just say aflutter?) and helped bring the field of behavioral investing into the spotlight. Their research demonstrated that the pain of loss is twice as strong as the joy of gain, and we act accordingly when making financial decisions. For example, consider the following two questions:

Nobel – Even though he collaborated with Tversky, only Kahneman received the Nobel Prize because Tversky died in 1996, and the Nobel Committee does not award prizes posthumously. Kahneman was the first true non-economist to receive the prize in economics. Alfred Nobel's will of 1895 provided money for prizes for achievement during the previous year in five categories: physics, chemistry, medical science or physiology, literature, and fraternity (furtherance of peace). After some early scientific discoveries were later discredited—such as Johannes Fibiger's award in 1926 for discovery of a parasite that caused cancer—the Nobel committees decided it might be better to let the honoree's work stand the test of time before selection, hence the almost two decades lag for Kahneman, and nearly three decades for Markowitz and Sharpe. Since a prize in economics was not included in Alfred Nobel's will it is not technically a Nobel Prize. In 1968, to celebrate its 300th anniversary, the Sveriges Riksbank donated a large sum of money to the Nobel Foundation to create the Nobel *Memorial* Prize in Economic Science in honor of Alfred Nobel.

1. You have $1,000 to invest and must choose one of two options:
   a) a sure gain of $500, or
   b) a 50% chance to gain $1,000 with a 50% chance to gain nothing.

2. You have $2,000 to invest and must choose one of two options:
   a) a sure loss of $500, or
   b) a 50% chance to lose $1,000 with a 50% chance to lose nothing.

The answers have the exact same results in both questions. If you chose a) you would walk away with $1,500 and if you chose b) you have a 50% chance of walking away with either $1,000 or $2,000. The difference is that one question is presented in a positive context (gain) and the other in a negative (loss).

When Kahneman and Tversky posed the same questions, 84% of respondents chose a) for the first question and 69% chose b) for the second. This is called loss aversion. Additional studies have confirmed that investors are twice as likely to sell winners, often prematurely, than they are to sell losers. We sell winners to avoid a potential loss should they head south, and when there is a loss (on paper), we postpone selling because we think if we can just hold on a little while longer it will come back, whereas if we actually sold, it would be a real loss and cause pain. Fear and greed are powerful emotions and should never be underestimated. (Some people mistakenly rationalize that if a stock has fallen 50% then went back up 50% they would break even, when in fact if it dropped 50% it would have to double to get back to where it was.)

A great example of our investment brains at work can be seen when looking at mutual fund

---

Bubbles – Isaac Newton was a really smart dude who gained fame and fortune by explaining gravity, creating his Laws of Motion and discovering calculus. He was an investor too, and just as susceptible to emotions as us less intelligent investors today.

The South Sea Company was founded in 1711 and was granted a monopoly on trade with the Spanish colonies in South America, and its stock price climbed. Being a smart fellow, in early 1720 Newton bought some shares at around £150. He sold a few months later at about £350 and made a tidy profit. Fueled by tales of South Seas riches the shares continued to soar and everyone was "making a killing." Isaac couldn't stand it any longer and jumped back in at around £700. By summer the shares reached £1,050 but when investors realized the South Sea Company couldn't deliver the expected results the speculative bubble burst. Newton sold his shares for a fraction of what he paid for them and lost £20,000 (about $1.72 million today) in the venture.

returns and the returns of those who invest in the funds. You would think they would be the same. Morningstar looked at the returns of 500 funds of all types and sizes over a 15 year period, and found that investor return was only 90% of fund return because of investors jumping in and out of the funds due to emotional reactions to market conditions or trying to time the market. Over the last twenty years investors have lost $122 billion because of these emotional reactions.

Other researchers looking at only large cap stocks (S&P 500) over a twenty year period ending in 2010, found that the stocks averaged a 9.1% return per year while the typical investor in those stocks earned just 3.8% annually. That's stupid crazy! It goes to show you, that the biggest threat to the average investor's portfolio is the average investor. Make your plan and sit tight. As famed investor Jack Bogle said when asked what investors should do during the 2000-2002 bear market: "Don't just do something, sit there." Smart dude that Bogle.

Dumb and Dumber – The emotions of fear and greed drive all markets and as Newton showed us, we're all susceptible to them. In the 1990s tech stocks exploded onto the market as people began to realize the potential of the intergalactic web and new companies with hyped potential sprang up everywhere. The valuation of many of these companies was astronomical even though they couldn't be supported by hard data and most of them owned nothing more than an idea. Younger Wall Street soothsayers proclaimed that this was the "new normal" and that the old rules didn't apply while the old-timers said a bubble was forming. I was skeptical and resisted getting into this game, but after a couple years of hearing how everyone was "making a killing" I jumped in. In less than a year I was up 30% and elated. How smart I was! Like all bubbles, the dot com bubble finally burst, most of the tech upstarts disappeared, and millions lost their shirts.

The following decade another bubble formed, this time in real estate. In some markets, like Las Vegas, Phoenix and on both coasts, home prices were going up nearly 50% a year and once again, after a couple years of everyone "making a killing", I took the plunge and bought a condo at the beach – with the same result. Trust me when I say that even after learning my lesson in the tech bubble, it was still very, very difficult to resist the siren call of big profits. It's the same psychology that has provided an unlimited supply of suckers for fraudsters throughout history. Remember, if it sounds too good to be true, stay away. Fortunately I stuck to my golden rule, which is to never invest more than 5% of your portfolio in any one company or industry. (In case you were wondering: I sold what was left of the tech stocks and took the hit. Ten years later the condo is still not worth what I paid for it but at least rental income covers most of the cost.) Does this make me twice as smart as Isaac Newton?

Here are a couple more reasons why we make irrational decisions:

Myopic Loss Aversion – Looking at a portfolio too often when the market is down causes us to be more conservative in order avoid potential loss. One study showed that investors who reviewed their portfolios monthly had a more conservative mix of 41% in stocks and 59% bonds, while those who reviewed annually had 70% in stocks and 30% in bonds.

Herd Mentality – If you're not confident in your investing strategy, you seek safety and validation by following the crowd, which is not always a good idea.

There is a lot of neurological science behind our behavior. It's long been known that logical thinking originates in the prefrontal cortex of the brain and it's been shown that people with injuries to the prefrontal cortex, as well as those with ADD, struggle with long-term financial decisions. Now researchers in the new field of neuroeconomics are discovering other parts of the brain that may be involved in Kahneman and Tversky's Prospect Theory. Maybe someday they'll come up with a "Buffett pill" that we could all take and be world class investors.

Mow the Grass

Some people like to work in the yard while others use a lawn service to mow the grass, plant flowers and trim the shrubs. It's not a matter of right or wrong, but simply a matter of choice. Just like Uncle Dick and Uncle Trev who we met earlier, some people have an interest in, or even passion for finances while others would rather sit and watch grass grow.

So this brings us back to the "know thyself" stuff. How you invest and with whom you invest should be driven by your circumstances and your personality. Everyone is different, so tailor your portfolio to your needs and tailor your risk to your personality. You have to know what type person you are and plan your approach to investing accordingly. The important thing is that you do something. Burying your head in the sand because you have no interest is not an option. Of course as we'll see, some ways of investing are a lot less expensive than others, which can mean more money in your pocket.

Selecting A Partner

If you have a company sponsored 401k plan, your employer determines many of the features in the plan, such as what investment options are available and if there will be an employee match. They also decide who will be managing the plan so you're stuck with whoever they choose. Some plans have low fees and offer lots of investment options while others don't. You can see how your plan stacks up at **brightscope.com**.

If you want to open a non-retirement investment account or an IRA, you'll need to open an account to hold your investments in, and for that you'll have several choices. Creating a portfolio that suits your needs can be as simple or as complex as you choose. You can make the decisions and do the work yourself or you can hire someone to do all or part of it for you. If you're going to hire someone to handle your account, you should be aware that the representative you chose will have to meet one of two standards:

The first is the *Suitability Standard,* which applies to stockbrokers. A broker, or broker/dealer must assess your situation and have a reasonable basis that his or her recommendations are *suitable* for you. For example, if you were 80 years old, wanted a portfolio to generate income and had a low tolerance for risk, it would be *suitable* to be in very conservative investments such as highly rated bonds and income producing stocks. However this standard does not necessarily require the investments that are *best* for you. If the broker had a choice of bonds that pay him or her a commission and others that did not, the broker would get the ones that paid the commission. That's how they make their money. While bonds would be deemed *suitable* for your portfolio these particular bonds would not necessarily be the *best* investment for you. This does not mean that brokers or anyone else following a suitability standard are crooks, it's just the way they get paid. However it may mean less money in your pocket and does provide an unscrupulous person greater opportunity to take advantage of a client so an extra degree of trust may be required.

A higher standard under the law is the *Fiduciary Standard* which requires investment advisors to place the client's interests above their own. In the above example, the advisor must select the bonds that do not pay them a commission. Registered Investment Advisers and Certified Financial Planners must follow the fiduciary standard. Since government regulators determined that brokers and insurance/annuity salespersons are "not to be deemed investment advisors" they are not held to this standard.

In 2010, the Dodd-Frank Act authorized the Security and Exchange Commission to require all financial advisors and brokers to follow the fiduciary standard, but due to intense lobbying from the banking, insurance and brokerage industries nothing was implemented. These groups contend that this action would force many small investors to pay more for retirement advice or preclude them from getting it altogether. In 2016 the Labor Department issued new rules that a fiduciary standard must be followed by anyone handling accounts subject to ERISA, such as IRAs and 401(k)s.

If the new administration doesn't do away with them, the rules are slated to take effect in April 2017 and will further muddy the investing waters, as some brokers are forced to wear two hats. They could be under the fiduciary standard when handling a client's retirement accounts and the suitability standard for the others. Should be interesting.

In addition to knowing the standard under which your potential account representative operates, you need to know how he or she gets paid. Today there are several ways people in the financial industry are compensated for their services:

Fee Only – Receives compensation only from the client; no commissions from mutual funds, insurance companies or brokerage firms. Investment advice is for a flat fee, usually an hourly rate but if you wanted the advisor to manage your portfolio, a fee based on the value of the assets managed is charged, usually between 0.3% and 2.5%. You can learn more about fee only planners at National Association of Personal Financial Advisors website (**napfa.org**) or the Garrett Planning Network (**garrettplanningnetwork.com**).

Commission Based – Income is entirely earned from commissions when you open an account or buy or sell financial products. This is the most common type of arrangement where you're dealing with a stockbroker from a brokerage company. Just remember that when someone is receiving a commission whenever you buy or sell a financial product and they only have to meet the suitability standard, there can be temptation to churn your account or put you into products that benefit them more than you. However, if you're going to work with your cousin Vinny, or someone you've known for years and trust explicitly, then have at it.

Fee Based – Receives fees from clients similar to fee-only advisors but also can make commissions from the sale of investment products.

Web Based – So called "robo advisors" are a recent but fast growing phenomena. They use proprietary programs based on MPT to create and manage low cost financial plans. Just as Turbo-Tax has replaced the CPA and online banking is replacing the bank teller, web-based advisors are becoming more popular, especially for entry level investors. Even traditional investment firms such as Charles Schwab and the Vanguard Group have gotten into the business. Clients enter financial particulars online and proprietary software

creates a plan. Some have a setup charge plus a monthly fee for ongoing monitoring while others charge a percentage of funds managed ranging from 0.25% to 0.8%. You can phone, chat or email if you wish to speak with someone but may not have one advisor assigned to you, and typically cannot trade on your account. Costs vary so compare several firms.

Fund companies – Another option is to open an account with a mutual fund company where a salaried account representative can guide you into constructing a portfolio that is appropriate for your particular situation. These accounts are usually self-directed, which means you will be doing the buying and selling of the stocks, bonds, and mutual funds in your account, however given what you're learning here, and the guidance and hand holding the representative provides, it's not that difficult. If you desire more personal attention, they can set you up with an affiliated fee-only advisor. As we'll see shortly however, not all mutual fund companies are created equal.

So your first step is to decide what type partner you want to hire. Ask friends and family for recommendations. Personally I believe you're best served by investing through a mutual fund company or hooking up with a fee only financial adviser, but if your cousin Vinny, who you grew up with, happens to be a stockbroker, that's okay too. Though it may cost you more, it's better to pay fees to someone than to do nothing.

When looking for a partner you should interview three or four candidates so you have a comparison. You're looking for someone you would be comfortable working with. Trust is very important. Have written questions ready when you go to the meeting such as:

- Outline your background, skills and education.
- How much experience do you have?

- What licenses and qualifications do you have?
- What services do you offer?
- When handling my account, are you a fiduciary?
- Will you be investing my money in individual stocks, bonds, mutual funds, or something else?
- How are you paid?
- Explain your fees.
- Where will my securities be held?
- In whose name will my investments be held?
- How often will I hear from you?

Expect the candidates you interview to ask questions of you too. At the very least they should ask you questions to determine your individual situation, such as:

- What is your investment objective?
- How old are you?
- What is your investment time horizon?
- What is your financial situation, income, net worth, tax bracket, etc?
- What is your tolerance for risk?

Alphabet Soup – People who offer financial advice usually have some letters following their names to indicate their qualifications, and as you might expect, some letters carry more weight than others. If you look up professional designations at finra.org you'll see a list of more than 150, so it can get really confusing. Some, like Certified Financial Planner (CFP), Chartered Financial Consultant (ChFC), Chartered Financial Analyst (ChFA), Certified Public Accountant (CPA) must have taken college level courses, have several years experience, and pass a rigorous exam. (A CPA might also have an additional Personal Financial Specialist credential.) Advisers such as these, who have spent years earning their designations are less likely to be scamming you and risking their careers.

Remember that anyone can have business cards printed. FINRA investigator Gerri Walsh said she has seen so called "financial professionals" whose business cards had HSG after their name, which it turns out stood for high school graduate. So whenever you see a bunch of letters after someone's name, take a minute to look them up.

Risk Tolerance

Investment professionals often employ questionnaires to assess your tolerance for risk so that they may do what's best or suitable for you, and to cover their behinds if you should get wild and crazy and stray too far from convention. Here are some typical questions:

1. Your trusted friend is a noted geologist and wants to put together an investment group to drill for oil. He says there is a 20% of hitting it big, in which case you would get 100 times the investment, but if it fails you'll lose everything. How much would you invest? Nothing, one month's salary, three month's salary, or six month's salary.

2. When you think of the word "risk" what comes to mind? Loss, uncertainty, opportunity or excitement.

3. You finished saving for your "dream vacation" and just before departure you lose your job. Would you: cancel the trip, take a cheaper trip, go as planned to have time to prepare for the upcoming job search, or upgrade to first class all the way, since it might be your last vacation in a long time.

You get the general idea of what they're looking for. You have to "know thyself" when it comes to saving money and it applies to investing too. You, and your advisor, need to tailor your investments to you. To help you do that, look at the following chart that shows returns based on six different allocation models, from an ultra-conservative 100% cash to a very aggressive 100% stocks, using data going back to 1926.

	Short Term	Conservative	Balanced	Growth	Agg Gth	Most Agge
Domestic Stk		14.00%	35.00%	49.00%	60.00%	70.00%
Int'l Stk		6.00%	15.00%	21.00%	25.00%	30.00%
Bonds		50.00%	40.00%	25.00%	15.00%	
Cash	100.00%	30.00%	10.00%	5.00%		
Best 1 Year	15.20%	31.06%	76.57%	109.55%	136.07%	162.89%
Best 5 Years	11.13%	17.24%	23.14%	27.27%	31.91%	36.12%
Worst 1 Year	-0.04%	-17.67%	-40.64%	-52.92%	-60.78%	-67.56%
Worst 5 Years	0.06%	-0.37%	-6.18%	-10.43%	-13.78%	-17.36%
Avg Return	3.58%	6.04%	7.90%	8.81%	9.42%	9.85%

We've already looked at how MPT can help your portfolio last longer, so now let's look at the risk side of investing. Instead of focusing on the best one or five year return (up 162% in one year—wow!) take a look at the worst one and five year returns to get a feel for your tolerance for risk. Would you lay awake at night if your 401(k) was down 40% for the year? How about if it were off by 67%? Would you freak out and sell everything? Knowing that there has never been a twenty year period where stocks have lost money, it's still a sometimes bumpy ride getting from year one to year 20, and you have to be able to sleep at night. That's the balancing act between risk and return.

When frugaler Anne Scheiber died at age 101, she still was 60% invested in stocks, which is rather aggressive for that age, however it is considered reasonable for someone in their 80's and beyond to maintain 20% to 40% in equities. We each have our own comfort level and you need to think about yours.

Fraudsters About

ATMs in certain parts of London post signs warning of "Fraudsters About," and likewise in the world of investing there can be crooks lurking. The first line of defense against these fraudsters is vigilance. To begin with, you should find the adviser, instead of the adviser finding you. Never do business with anyone who calls you out of the blue, or emails you with an "incredible opportunity, but only if you act now."

While there are real threats, you should know that the overwhelming majority of financial professionals are honest and aboveboard, and they work hard because they know they'll lose you as a client if you're not happy. I know many and would trust them without reservation. Odds are very slim that you will ever be caught up in any sort of Ponzi scheme, plus most accounts are insured up to $500,000 against broker fraud. However when it comes to your hard earned cash you must still exercise due diligence when selecting a partner. As Ronald Reagan said when negotiating with the Soviets, "trust but verify." So once you find someone you're comfortable with, check out him or her and the firm they work for with the Financial Industry Regulatory Authority at FINRA.org/Brokercheck, and with your state's securities regulator at **nasaa.org** (click on the tab "contact your regulator"). Another place to check out financial advisers is **BrightScope.com**. (See: Prisoner #61727-054 sidebar, next page.)

Mutual Funds

A mutual fund is a professionally managed investment vehicle that invests pooled money collected from investors to buy stocks, bonds, and other investments. It is usually part of a mutual fund company that has many funds under one brand name, which is referred to as a mutual fund family. There are thousands of funds and hundreds of fund families. A large fund company can have more than one hundred funds in the family.

Some fund companies sell only through brokers or other agents and charge commissions, while others allow you to open an account directly with the fund. (Vanguard, Fidelity, Schwab, TIAA, T. Rowe Price are a few examples of fund companies that allow direct investing.)

If you have an account with one fund company you are usually not limited to that company's funds and can buy thousands of funds from many other fund companies too. Sometimes however fund companies are in competition with each other and will charge a one time transaction fee if you want a rival's fund for your account. For example, if you have an account with Fidelity and want to buy a Vanguard fund, there will be a charge.

> **Prisoner #61727-054** – Bernie grew up in a Jewish family in New York City. After high school he attended the University of Alabama for one year before transferring to Hofstra University where he graduated in 1960, with a degree in political science. That same year, with $5,000 he made as a sprinkler installer and lifeguard, he started Madoff Investment Securities and began selling penny stocks. He soon got into other investments, and using connections in the Jewish community, Madoff promised outsized gains, which he delivered with phony statements to defraud investors (Larry King, Sandy Koufax, Phyllis George, and John Malkovich among others), hospitals, and charities. This "affinity fraud" caused his clients to turn a blind eye to any possibility of wrongdoing, even though throughout the scam, several big red flags appeared that investors and even regulators refused to see. Eventually Bernie stopped making any investments at all, putting incoming money directly into his bank account, and would rob-Peter-to-pay-Paul whenever clients needed withdrawals. His Ponzi scheme bilked thousands of investors out of tens of billions of dollars and went on for decades.
>
> You should be aware that independent financial advisers typically hold securities with third party security firms in the client's name and have authority only to trade those investments and never to withdraw funds. These third-party companies send out monthly or quarterly statements and allow you to access your account online so you can follow investment changes. Madoff held the investments in-house and generated his own bogus statements. *Big red flag!* Also, a firm with assets of this size should have had a large, nationally recognized accounting firm audit the books with a team of CPAs every year. Madoff hired a close personal friend in a three-person accounting firm (only one of whom was an accountant) to do the job. Another big flag. With these giant warning signs you have to wonder how he could pull this off for so long. Since 2009, Mr. Madoff has resided in a "gated community" outside of Raleigh, N.C.

But since there are usually so many funds to chose from, this is usually not an issue. All funds have names and trade under a five letter ticker symbol ending in X. Back in the day, when they actually used ticker tape (think "Daddy" Warbucks in Little Orphan Annie), New York Stock Exchange stocks had one, two or three letter symbols, NASDAQ had four, and when mutual funds came along, they stuck an X on the end to distinguish them from other securities.

The main advantage of a mutual fund is that small investors can buy into a diversified, professionally managed investment portfolio that they otherwise might not be able to afford or be capable of managing. Broadly speaking, funds invest in stocks, bonds, cash or some combination of all three, so let's take a look at the most common types.

Equity Funds (Stocks)

Domestic Funds invest in U.S. companies and can cover all parts of the Morningstar style box from stable, dividend paying large companies to more volatile small ones. Growth companies that emphasize capital appreciation, under-priced value companies, or a blend of both types can be found in these funds. They provide a good base for any portfolio.

International Funds invest in companies outside the U.S. and can concentrate on most of the globe or a particular region such as Europe, the Pacific, and Latin America, or even a single country. Some also focus on particular types of countries such as emerging markets. So-called global or world funds include American companies. International funds can bring diversification to a portfolio.

Sector Funds invest in just one industry such as banking, gold, and natural gas, or one sector of the market such as energy, natural resources, and utilities. Sector funds lack diversification and are more volatile.

Fixed Income Funds (Bonds)

Taxable Bond Funds can include bonds of the U.S. Government or corporate bonds, and can cover the Morningstar style box from both long and short term, and from highest quality to high yield "junk." These funds should be part of a balanced portfolio.

Municipal Bond Funds invest in bonds from state and local governments that are exempt from federal, and sometimes state taxes. Often used when there are tax considerations.

International Bond Funds invest in corporate and government bonds outside the U.S.

and allow further diversification, but like international equity funds can incur currency risk and, depending on the country involved, substantial credit risk.

Money Market Funds invest in high quality, short term fixed-income securities and are considered by many to be the same as cash. Money market funds attempt to maintain a net asset value of $1.00 per share, meaning investors never have a capital gain or loss but only earn interest income. If a money market fund ever fails to maintain the $1.00 per share value it is said to "break the buck" and can trigger panic among shareholders since this safe-as-cash investment is not FDIC insured like bank deposits. This has only happened twice in history.

Hybrid Funds

Balanced Funds provide a mixture of safety and capital appreciation through a balanced weighting of stocks and bonds; typically 60% stocks and 40% bonds. A related fund, known as an asset allocation fund, has a similar objective but allows the fund manager more leeway in adjusting the mix to fit economic conditions. These funds usually provide less risk than a pure equity fund and a greater return than a pure bond fund. A lot like Markowitz and Sharpe's Modern Portfolio Theory.

Target/Life Cycle Funds are similar to balanced funds except the managers adjust the asset mix of stocks, bonds and cash to fit a future date. The funds are named in five year increments such as 2020, 2025, 2030, etc. An investor who is planning to retire in say 2044, would invest in a 2045 fund, and the stock/bond/cash mix would become more conservative as that year got closer. These target date funds are often offered in 401(k) plans. More on them shortly.

Fund of Funds (FOF) is a type of mutual fund made up of other funds, usually but not always within the same family. Instead of buying individual stocks and bonds, the fund manager buys stock funds and bond funds to get the desired allocation. Fees are often higher than single manager funds, depending on the management fees of the underlying funds. Several FOF's came under question after losing money when they invested in a fund run by Bernie Madoff. Wow! Where was their due diligence?

Specialty Funds

Socially-Responsible Funds invest in companies that meet the criteria of a particular belief. Their origins go back to the Quakers in 1758, who prohibited members from investing in the slave trade. Today more than 400 funds apply moral, environmental, ethical, religious, or human rights filters to limit investments in certain industries, with pornography, alcohol, gambling, weapons, animal testing, and tobacco being the most common. Returns on most of these funds are on par with non-socially-responsible funds, but they usually have higher expenses. These funds have had their own index called the Domini 400 Social Index.

<u>Index Funds</u> invest in the stocks or bonds that make up a particular index. For example, the S&P 500 is an index consisting of the 500 largest publicly traded companies in the U.S., so a S&P 500 Index fund would simply buy shares in those companies, which can pretty much be done by a computer. Index funds are called passively managed funds, because they just mimic an index and are therefore much less labor intensive which keeps operating cost extremely low. An actively managed fund on the other hand, would need a staff of analysts to decide which stocks or bonds to include in the fund and would be continually buying and selling securities in an attempt to beat the fund's benchmark.

Indexes

Mutual funds are also classified as "load" or "no-load." A load is a one time sales commission payable when you purchase (front load) or sell (back-end load) a mutual fund. If you wanted to buy $10,000 of a fund with a 5% front end load you would actually buy $9,500 of the fund and give $500 to whoever sold it to you. A no-load fund is just what it sounds like: there is no sales charge. While there are many fine mutual funds with loads, there are no studies that show they are superior to no-load funds and I see no reason to ever buy one. However, even some no-load funds may have a redemption fee for the first few months to discourage speculators from frequently trading in and out of the fund. All funds have administrative, operating and sometimes marketing fees. Collectively these fees are referred to as the "expense ratio" and can have a large impact on a funds return, so just remember, lower is better. All fees are required to be disclosed to potential buyers in the fund's prospectus.

Various publications rank fund families and here, in alphabetical order, is a short list of some no-load, low-cost fund families which are always among the best.

Charles Schwab – Offers a full range of investment products and services. Schwab has the most company owned and franchised retail branches throughout the United States. They have offices in most major cities if face-to-face contact is important to you.

Fidelity – Founded in 1946, it is one of the behemoths of the industry. It's noted for its research and is a big player in retirement services. They offer a huge selection of both actively managed and index funds, plus ETFs of their own and from other families. Like most fund families, Fidelity is itself a publicly traded company and advertises heavily to attract new business and grow profits.

T. Rowe Price – Founded in 1937 and known for its broad range of quality no-load mutual funds. Only a couple offices outside the Baltimore – Washington D.C. area, so most business is done online or on the phone.

Vanguard – The largest mutual fund company and king of low fee index funds. Unusual among fund companies, Vanguard is owned by the investors in it's mutual funds, much like a credit union is owned by depositors, so it doesn't pander to the corporate bottom line and can usually offer the lowest fees.

The World is Your Oyster

After World War II, the United States was the only major country that had not suffered heavy damage, so our economy was humming along building everything from houses to automobiles to washing machines for returning GIs and the rest of the world. We were pretty much the only game around when it came to investing.

Today, only 26% of the world's publicly traded companies are in the U.S.; 80% of world

---

Bogle – John "Jack" Bogle grew up in a well to do family that lost everything in the Great Depression. He worked his way through Princeton and graduated magna cum laude with a degree in economics in 1951. His senior thesis was about the nascent mutual fund industry and he concluded that expenses and fees were too high, and mutual funds "can make no claim to superiority over the market averages."

After graduation he went to work for Wellington Management Company, a firm that actively managed investments for individuals and mutual funds, and by age 39, was CEO. For 23 years Bogle lauded the advantages of actively managed portfolios but in 1974, after pushing through a merger that failed, he was fired and in what he calls his "epiphany," went back to the premise of his senior thesis. He founded the Vanguard Group and launched the first index fund, which now is called the Vanguard 500 Index. Today Vanguard is the largest mutual fund company in the world and specializes in low cost index funds, and Jack Bogle has thousands of "Bogleheads" in chapters around the world following his philosophy. (Go to **bogleheads.org**)

GDP comes from outside the U.S., and a foreign stock market has outperformed ours in every one of the last 30 years. In other words, there's a whole big world out there that you shouldn't neglect when it comes to putting together your portfolio. But keep in mind that large cap American companies do about half their business overseas which gives you some exposure. Nonetheless, international investments should be part of the mix.

Morningstar*

Founded in 1984, Morningstar Inc. provides investment research data. They are noted for creating the style boxes for categorizing stocks and bonds that we looked at earlier, but they are most famous to average investors for their Morningstar Rating™ star rating system for mutual funds. They assign from one to five stars, based on historical performance, in dozens of different categories. This is a "backward looking" system and studies in the 1990s showed there was no predictive value to these ratings, so in 2002 they tweaked their methodology, then rejiggered it again in 2012.

Newer studies show some moderate predictive power, with the strongest predictive value for lower rated funds, indicating that one and two star funds were more likely to continue their poor performance in the future.

Here's how the star system works: The bottom 10% of funds receive one star, the next 22.5% two stars, the middle 35% three stars, the next 22.5% four stars and the top 10% five stars. In 2011 Morningstar launched a "forward looking" rating system to compliment their star system with gold, silver, bronze and neutral ratings, but it's too soon to know its predictive value.

Every mutual fund stresses in their prospectus that "past performance is no guarantee of future results" and every investor needs to keep that in mind. The Morningstar Rating™ system is but one of many screening tools and you should never buy a fund based solely on it's star rating, but it might be a reasonable idea to stay away from funds with only one or two stars. Interestingly however, while everyone searches for the holy grail to allow them to predict winners and losers, Morningstar's own studies have shown that the best predictor of future performance, in every asset class and over all time periods is the expense ratio – the lower the fees, the better the performance. End of story.

Exchange Traded Funds (E. T. Fs)

An ETF is a mutual fund that usually tracks an index and trades like a stock. A mutual fund sets its value at the end of each trading day, by dividing the value of the assets in the fund by the number of fund shares outstanding. But an ETF's price fluctuates throughout the day as it is bought and sold, and just like a stock. To redeem your shares you must find a buyer in the open market. Also like stocks, ETFs can be sold short and buyers pay a commission. Because they are mimicking an index, ETFs have much lower expense ratios than actively managed mutual funds, and since they don't have to redeem shares at the end of the trading day, they are often more tax efficient.

When ETFs started in 1993, they followed traditional indexes such as the S&P 500 but have since exploded in popularity, and now there are more than 1,500 of them; many that are narrowly focused and make little sense for investors. Today you can find ETF's for currencies, agricultural products, metals, and a host of other things. It's gone a little crazy.

Building Your Portfolio

So after all the theories, history and background babble, you're probably chomping at the bit for it to end and to get to the actual investing part. (Or maybe you just need some beer.) How do I decide on asset allocation? Where the heck am I supposed to put my money? Let's get to it.

The Empire – The sun never set on the British Empire because it was so damn big. The Brits had colonists and troops all over the world but there were more in India than anywhere else. So what's the one thing expats want when far from home – that would be beer. One problem back in the 19th century was it was an 11,000 mile journey that took two months. (This was decades before the French started digging the ditch from Suez to the Red Sea.)

Burton-on-Trent was an English beer town famous for their October beer, a well hopped pale ale that was meant to be aged. In March 1822, Tsar Alexander I of Russia slapped a tariff on all British imports and put the hurt on the brewers in Burton-on-Trent. The East India Company saw an opportunity and in 1827 arranged for the shipment of several hogsheads of strongly hopped pale ale to India. The venture was a success and by 1840 *India Pale Ale* had become popular in England itself. When one door closes, another one usually opens. (A Hogshead was a large cask that could hold 1,000 pounds of tobacco or 145 gallons of beer. There was also a smaller wine hogshead that held 79 gallons.)

In a military sense, strategy is how you plan the war, and tactics are how you fight the battle, so think of strategy as the big picture while tactics are on a lesser scale. The tactical is no less important than the strategic. When investing, think of the strategic part as asset allocation, which means how much of your portfolio you allocate to stocks, bonds, cash or other assets. Within your portfolio you must also diversify among various types and classes of stocks, bonds and other assets. This diversification, and how it changes over time, is the tactical.

As the economy and your own situation changes, re-balancing and tactical tweaking of your portfolio may become necessary to maintain the desired asset mix or adjust to conditions. How much of the strategic and tactical you get into depends on how you elect to proceed. If you choose to hire a fee-based, or web based advisor, they'll be doing all the work for you. But if you want to save some money and do it yourself, we'll take a look look at four options, beginning with the easiest and progressing to the most labor intensive and time consuming, for you to consider.

Option One – Target Funds

If everything you've read so far has made your eyes glaze over, and you'd rather go rearrange your sock drawer, THIS IS THE MOMENT YOU'VE BEEN WAITING FOR. Here is the hassle free strategy I promised you at the beginning of the chapter.

Were you ever up late at night channel surfing, and came across an infomercial with Ron "Ronco" Popiel pitching his rotisserie oven? Every time he put a roast or chicken or some vegetable in the rotisserie he said "Set it and forget it," and the audience in unison parroted back a loud, "Set it and forget it." After 30 minutes of this, the "Set it and forget it" mantra was stuck in your head, which I suppose was good marketing for him but didn't really help much with your insomnia.

Well, target funds are the "set it and forget it" investment option for those who don't want to spend any time deciding on asset allocation or managing a portfolio. As I wrote a couple pages ago, these are balanced funds that become more conservative as your retirement date gets closer. To see target funds in action, I've selected some of the low cost players in this arena so you can get a look at how your money would be allocated if you put it in a fund for the year 2055, compared to a fund for the year 2020.

	% Domestic Stock	% Int'l Stock	% Bonds	% Cash
Vanguard 2055	54	36	10	0
T. Rowe Price 2055	56	31	10	3
Schwab 2055	64	29	2	5
Fidelity 2055	66	28	5	1
Average	60	31	7	2
Vanguard 2020	35	22	41	2
T. Rowe Price 2020	40	21	36	3
Schwab 2020	37	14	41	8
Fidelity 2020	43	21	30	6
Average	39	20	37	5

As you can see, for a young working person who is going to retire sometime around the year 2055, the asset allocation averages 91% stocks (60% domestic plus 31% international), 7% bonds and 2% cash. This allows someone with such a long time horizon to take advantage of the greater long-term potential of the stock market. Now look at the allocation for someone who is about to retire and is in the 2020 target date fund. The mix has shifted to a much more conservative 59% stocks, 37% bonds and 5% cash. Even after retirement the allocation in these funds continues to shift and eventually ends up with about 40% stocks, 40% bonds and 20% cash.

In a target fund, not only do the managers adjust the asset allocation of stocks, bonds and cash as retirement draws closer, they also do the tactical tweaking, and change the domestic/international stock mix and duration of the bonds as needed. Some critics say this one-size-fits-all approach fails to account for the different risk tolerances of investors, and that may be true, however, you can tweak it and be a little more or less conservative by simply selecting a fund with an earlier or later date. Many 401(k) plans offer target fund choices but if yours does not, you can build your own using index funds.

Set It and Forget It! – Pitchman Ron Popiel, founder of Ronco, has probably logged more infomercial time on late night television than the famous Billy Mayes. Born in 1935, Popiel's parents divorced when he was very young, and he spent several years of his youth in foster homes in upstate New York. Around age seven his grandparents rescued him and his brother from foster care and took them to Florida. At age 17 they moved to Chicago where Ron was eventually reunited with his father Samuel, an inventor who sold his gadgets through chain stores like Woolworth, Sears and Walgreens. Soon he was hawking gadgets on the streets of Chicago that he had bought wholesale from his father.

An inventor himself, Ron made his first television commercial in the mid 1950s and by the 1960s he was off the streets and selling his Pocket Fishermen, Ronco Spray Gun, Chop-O-Matic, Veg-O-Matic, and Showtime Rotisserie to late night audiences. In 2005, Popiel sold his company for $55 million and retired to Beverly Hills.

Option Two – Index Funds

Should your 401k plan not offer target funds or you just want to be a bit more hands on and save some money, but don't need it to become a second job, then index funds are a simple and easy choice. A great argument can be made that this is the best investment strategy, but it does take a little more work. We know that fees matter, especially over time, and since index funds have the lowest expense ratio, you'll save by building a simple portfolio using these funds.

The exact allocation of stocks and bonds is up to you and your tolerance for risk, but the target funds above offer a good starting point. Let's say you were thinking of buying a 2055 target fund that was 90% in stocks (half domestic and half international) and 10% in bonds and it had an expense ratio of 0.75%. Instead, you could put 45% of your money into a U.S. total stock market index fund, 45% in an international index fund, and the remaining 10% into a total bond market index fund and get the same asset allocation but have an expense ratio of less than 0.1%.

Rules – The 10,000 hour rule – Based on research by psychologist K. Anders Ericsson and made famous in Malcolm Gladwell's book *Outliers: The Story of Success*, this rule says mastery of just about anything can be achieved with 10,000 hours practice. At 90 minutes a day it'll take you 20 years, so get started.

Rule of 72: To determine approximately how many years it will take an investment to double simply divide the interest rate into 72. For example, an investment paying 8% per year would take about 9 years to double (72/8 = 9). And to see what return you would need for a particular time period just reverse the process – to double my investment in 5 years would require about a 14.4% rate of return (72/5=14.4). This gets you in the ballpark. To be more exact when dealing with compounding interest, some math gurus say to use 69.3 instead of 72, but who wants to try those mental gymnastics?

Pareto 80/20 Rule – More than 100 years ago Italian economist Vilfredo Pareto noticed that 20% of the pea pods in his garden produced 80% of the peas. He then noticed that 80% of the land was owned by 20% of the people and after further research formulated his principle on the uneven distribution of just about everything. His principle is used today in mathematics, manufacturing, politics, software, safety, and dozens of other areas. For example: 80% of traffic occurs 20% of the time; 20% of computer bugs cause 80% of the crashes; 20% of workers produce 80% of results; 80% of a teachers time is taken up by 20% of the students; and on and on and on. Basically it means life isn't fair.

You might think it's no big deal to lower your expense ratio from three quarters of one percent to one tenth of a percent, but over time it's a huge savings. The only thing is, now you will be responsible for re-balancing your portfolio. This is easy peasy. Don't let it intimidate you.

Sometimes equities are better performers and sometimes bonds are doing better, that's why we have some of each, and over time you may find that your portfolio gets a little out of balance and needs your attention. Let's say the U.S. market has been down and international stocks and bonds have been up and your mix has gone from your desired 45%/45%/10% allocation to 37%/50%/13%. All you have to do is go online to your account and sell some of the bond and international funds and buy a little more of the domestic stock fund. Think about it, this is buying low (domestic stocks) and selling high (international stocks and bonds), exactly what you should be doing. Don't get too carried away with re-balancing however, once or twice a year is plenty. I actually do it when things get out of balance by 4% or 5%, rather than by the calendar.

Option Three – Actively Managed Funds

A portfolio of actively managed funds takes considerably more work and will certainly have higher fees, but a lot of people go this route because they enjoy it and just know in their heart-of-hearts they can beat the indexes. Once you decide on your asset allocation, you're going to have to analyze funds to make choices. When you first open your account ask the representative to walk you through the process on their website. I can't describe the procedure exactly because each company's website is different, but it's not as difficult as it sounds, and once you get familiar with the website, it gets easier.

For example, in the equity portion of your account you'll need to look for large cap, small cap and international funds, so go to your fund family website and find the mutual fund research section. Select large cap funds and you should get some filters to winnow things down. It will give you a list of choices. If the list is too long, tighten up your parameters. Pick a few with the lowest expense ratio and lowest turnover ratio. Then, if you're not feeling comfortable, call or visit your account representative for his or her feedback on your efforts. You'll need to do the same for small cap and international, and for the elements of your bond allocation. One strategy some people use to lighten the work load is to create a hybrid mix of half index and half managed funds.

Time for a pop quiz. Look at the following data from two different periods and answer this question: If you were buying a bond fund in each period, would you want a long- or short-term bond fund?

	1980-1982	2010-2015
Prime interest rate	21.5% (peak)	3.25% (bottom)

If this makes perfect sense to you then you might feel comfortable doing some tactical adjusting of your bond funds, and be okay with a portfolio that includes actively managed funds. However, if this makes your head hurt, and you'd rather shotgun an IcySlush to induce a brain freeze rather than even think about it, you should be in a target fund or a few broad index funds. (The answer: Buy long term bonds when rates peaked in the 80s and shorter term when rates hit bottom. Remember, if you have a long term bond fund and rates decline, the value of your fund will go up more.)

Option Four – Individual Stocks

If you choose to use individual stocks and bonds, it becomes more time consuming and labor intensive to construct a portfolio with proper asset allocation and diversification. It's fairly easy to establish the desired allocation of stocks, bonds and cash but maintaining diversification can be challenging. You have to pick stocks in so many categories that it

---

Enron – You never want to put more than 5% of your investment assets in any one stock, even if it's the company you work for. Enron Corporation was a highly regarded global energy giant and for six years in a row, from 1996 to 2001, was named "America's Most Innovative Company" by Fortune Magazine. In 1995, it established the Enron Prize for Distinguished Public Service, awarding it to such notables as Colin Powell, Mikhail Gorbachev, and Nelson Mandela. In 2000, it was on Fortune's list of "100 Best Companies to Work for in America." The company provided a 401(k) plan and generously matched employees contributions with Enron stock. This was one great corporate citizen and a wonderful place to work—or so everyone thought.

It turns out they were cooking the books and incurring massive losses. In January 2001, when everything came to light, Enron stock was trading at more than $80 a share and within a year was trading at less than 80 cents per share. Throughout the slide, management encouraged employees to hold on to their shares, insisting they were undervalued. CEO Ken Lay claimed the stock was worth $130 and encouraged employees to buy more while he and other executives were secretly selling their own shares as the company slid toward bankruptcy. Many workers bought into his BS. Workers with less than five years of service or less than 50 years of age were not allowed to sell their Enron shares in the 401(k) accounts and were wiped out. Lay and COO Jeffrey Skilling were found guilty of multiple felonies but Lay died of a heart attack before sentencing. Skilling presently resides in a "gated community" in Montgomery, Alabama, serving a 14 year sentence.

will tax your time and brain.

You will need to select and monitor large and small cap, plus value and growth stocks. Then you'll want exposure to energy, financial, consumer, industrial, health-care, communications, utilities and all that stuff. In the bond arena you'll need a mix of long-term, short-term, government, corporate, foreign, domestic, mortgage backed, investment grade and junk bonds. Pretty soon it's like herding cats and unless you have extensive financial experience and lots of time on your hands, it can be difficult for one person. I don't recommend it, but if you want to go in this direction don't do it alone, work with a professional.

Dollar Cost Averaging (D.C.A.)

DCA is an investment strategy that reduces volatility and mitigates risk by automatically investing a fixed amount of money on a regular time schedule (weekly, monthly, quarterly, etc.) regardless of what the market is doing. This results in your average cost per share being less than the average price per share of the investment. Let's say you invest $500 every month into shares of a mutual fund. If the price of the fund falls you end up buying more shares, and if the price rises you get fewer shares for your fixed monthly investment. Here's what it looks like over a six month period.

DATE	AMOUNT	PRICE/SHARE	# SHARES
January	$500.00	$50.00	10
February	$500.00	$45.04	11.1
March	$500.00	$40.00	12.5
April	$500.00	$42.02	11.9
May	$500.00	$47.16	10.6
June	$500.00	$53.19	9.4
Total	$3,000.00		65.5
Avg Price /Share		$46.23	
Your Avg Cost/Share		$45.80	

As you can see, the average cost you paid per share is $45.80 ($3,000/65.5), yet the average price per share is $46.23 over the six month period. After six months the $3,000 you put in would be worth $3484 (65.5 shares x $53.19). If you had instead made a lump-sum purchase of $3000 in January, by June you would have $3,191 (60 shares x $53.19).

However, those who don't believe in DCA argue that in a rising market you would be

DATE	AMOUNT	PRICE/SHARE	# SHARES
January	$500.00	$50.00	10
February	$500.00	$50.00	10
March	$500.00	$54.94	9.1
April	$500.00	$55.55	9
May	$500.00	$60.24	8.3
June	$500.00	$62.50	8
Total	$3,000.00		54.4
Avg Price /Share		$55.54	
Your Avg Cost/Share		$55.15	

better off investing a lump sum at the beginning instead of periodic amounts, and they're right. Let's change the numbers a little and take a look:

In this example, after six months of DCA your $3,000 would have grown to $3,400 (54.4 shares x $62.50) but if you had made a $3,000 lump-sum purchase in January, by June it would be $3,750 (60 shares x $62.50). Of course, that requires the clairvoyance of an Oda Mae Brown (*Ghost*) because you just don't know for sure if and when the market is going up. With DCA, whether it's a rising or falling market, you end up paying slightly less than the average price for your shares.

Perhaps the best part of dollar cost averaging is not the mathematical, but the psychological aspect of the whole thing. By having set up an automatic $500 monthly investment you're actually doing something, and not sitting on the sidelines waiting for the perfect time to buy (sounds like timing to me), plus you get to sleep a little better at night because should the share price fall, you can take some comfort in the fact that your $500 is able to buy more shares.

The Tax Man Cometh

Tax avoidance is using the law to get every tax break you deserve, and is perfectly legal. Tax evasion is cheating on your taxes. That's illegal and is what the Feds used to send Al Capone off to a gated community in Atlanta in 1931. Orange is definitely not the new black, and you don't want to go there!

If you look at the chart at the beginning of this

chapter you can see that investing in stocks gives you the biggest bang for your buck over the long term and is the best way to reach your long term goals. If you had invested $1 in the stock market in 1926, it would have grown to around $4,700 by 2014. If you had put that dollar in bonds it would have grown to about $100 and if you stuck it in the bank it would be worth about $22.

The beauty of retirement accounts is that they are sheltered from Uncle Sam, but when you're investing outside of retirement accounts you must take tax consequences into consideration. The returns shown on the chart at the beginning of this chapter are without taxes. If you had to pay taxes each year from 1926, that $1 investment in stocks would have grown to about $950 instead of $4,700 and your $1 bond investment would be worth around $20 instead of $110. Wow! That's a chunk of change going from your pocket to Uncle Sam's. Fund that 401k and IRA! It's a no brainer.

Some investments are more tax efficient than others. When a mutual fund sells a stock within the fund that has increased in value there is a capital gain, and that is passed along to the shareholders of the fund. So even though you have not sold any of your shares in the fund for a profit, come tax time you will still have to pay taxes for the capital gain that occurred because of trading within the fund. The less buying and selling of stocks within the fund, the more tax efficient it is. This is known as the turnover ratio. When you are searching for funds for a non-retirement account those with lower turnover ratios are the better deal if all other considerations are equal. That's another reason index funds are usually a better bet – there's virtually no turnover.

Easy Eddie's Legacy – Edward "Easy Eddie" O'Hare was a mob lawyer in Chicago who worked for Al Capone. In 1930, to save his own skin, he turned against Capone and began providing information to the feds, which helped convict the mobster. In 1939, a week before Capone was to be released from prison, Eddie was assassinated while leaving the Sportsman Park racetrack in his Lincoln-Zephyr.

Eddie left behind a son called "Butch" who had graduated from the Naval Academy and was a pilot in the Pacific. In February 1942, Butch found himself as the sole aircraft between the USS Lexington and an inbound formation of nine Japanese heavy bombers. He immediately attacked, shooting down three and damaging two more enemy aircraft, saving his ship from certain damage or even loss, and became the first naval aviator to receive the Medal of Honor. In November 1943, Lieutenant Commander Edward "Butch" O'Hare, lead the first-ever carrier-launched night mission to intercept enemy torpedo bombers and went missing. The Navy named a destroyer after him and back home in Chicago, in 1949, local Orchard Field was renamed O'Hare International Airport in his honor.

This probably does not apply to most Millennials but someday it might so I'll throw a few words at it. Some people invest part of the bond portion of their non-retirement portfolio in municipal bonds (called muni's) and depending on your tax bracket it can be a good move. A tax bracket is a range of incomes taxed at a given rate, so in our progressive tax system, the higher the income, the higher the tax rate. (A single person making up to $9,225 is in the 10% federal tax bracket while someone making more than $413,000 would be in the 39.6% tax bracket.)

Muni bonds are exempt from federal taxes and sometimes state taxes. To see if they might be right for your portfolio, you need to determine the tax equivalent yield. For instance, if a muni paid 4% interest and taxable bonds were paying 5%, which would you choose? To find out, you divide the muni yield by 1 minus your tax bracket. If you are in the 10% bracket, you divide 4 by .9 (1- .10) and get a tax equivalent yield of 4.44%, so you would better off getting the taxable bond. But if you were in the 39.6% bracket the tax equivalent yield would be 6.62% (4 divided by 0.604) a really good deal. That's why Daddy Warbucks liked them.

Other Forms of Investing

Rejection – After graduating from Florida State, Sara Blakely intended to go to law school but had failed the LSAT, twice. So she auditioned to play Goofy at Disney World but she wasn't tall enough, so they hired her as a chipmunk. During her three months at Disney she also tried to make it as a stand-up comic without much success. Blakely then moved on to selling fax machines door-to-door where she found she had a flair for sales despite having a lot of doors slammed in her face. Required to wear pantyhose in the hot Florida sun Sara disliked the appearance of the seam on the foot when she wore open-toed shoes. So she experimented by cutting the feet off of her pantyhose, but that created another problem when the pantyhose rolled up her legs.

In 1998, at age 27, Sara was transferred to Atlanta and spent nights and weekends over the next two years, plus $5,000 of her savings perfecting her idea of footless pantyhose and writing her own patent. She then drove to North Carolina where, after being turned down by numerous hosiery mills, she finally found someone to make a prototype. Sara returned home to design the packaging and decide what to call her product. She settled on the name Spanx and applied for a trademark. After seven years of selling fax machines she quit and launched her business. By 2012, at age 41, Sara Blakely became the youngest female billionaire in the world. You go girl!

Invest in Yourself – Small business is the backbone of America. There are 5.7 million private sector businesses in the US and 99% of them have fewer than 500 employees. (89% have fewer than 20 employees.) While Walmart employs 1.4 million and the likes of McDonald's, IBM, Home Depot, and other giant companies employ hundreds of thousands, about half of all jobs are in small business, as are more than 60% of the new jobs created.

A majority of first generation millionaires are self-employed. They are entrepreneurs who own dry cleaners, plumbing supply stores, real estate offices, pest control services, machine shops, and a host of other small businesses. They work long hours, drive used cars, wear off the rack suits, live in middle class houses, value education for their children, live below their means, and are usually prolific savers.

If you want to go down this road and start a small business, it's a good idea to dip your toe in the water first by getting a job in the area you're considering just to see what it's really like and learn the ropes a bit. Even if you have a can't miss idea for a new widget or better way of doing something, don't quit your day job untill you've done your homework and got all your ducks lined up, then go for it. Slow and steady usually wins this race.

Real Estate – It has been said that more millionaires have been made investing in real estate than the stock market. One big advantage that investing in real estate affords is the concept of leverage. Let's look at Bubba and his sister one more time. After suffering from internet addiction disorder they both had to retire from the circus. For a while Bubbette hooked up with a Cajun trapeze artist named Junior, but it didn't work out so he went back to the bayou and she joined her brother in Sarasota to do some investing.

Bubba invested $40,000 in the stock market and in two years made a 10% return on his investment, which he then sold, for a before tax profit of $4,000. His sister also had $40,000 to invest and used it for a 10% down payment on a $400,000 ranch house that she rented to some retired clowns. After two years the value of the house also went up 10% (to $440,000) so Bubbette sold and realized a before tax profit of $40,000. That's leverage.

The downside of leverage is that Bubbette was in a potentially riskier position than her brother. If the clowns didn't pay the rent or the roof sprung a leak, Bubbette was on the hook for it. If Bubba's investment lost half its value he would be down $20,000, but if Bubbette's investment lost half its value, she would be down $200,000. Ouch! The housing bubble of 2006 saw prices decline by more than 50% in some parts of the country and a lot of investors lost their properties or ended up in bankruptcy. That said, real estate can be a great investment vehicle if you know what you're doing and don't get overextended.

Another benefit of owning real estate is that you get to shelter some of the income from the tax man. Expenses in maintaining a property are tax deductible plus you get to write off a portion of the value of the property, called depreciation, over time. This may give you a legitimate tax loss, even when the property is paying you money each month.

If you'd like to add some real estate to your portfolio without becoming a hands-on landlord, you can invest in a Real Estate Investment Trust or REIT (pronounced "reet").

From Watches to Houses – Entrepreneurship is a big part of what made this country great. In 1880, seventeen year old Richard Sears went to work for the railroad as a telegraph operator for the Minneapolis and St. Louis Railway, and by age 23 was a station agent. When a shipment of gold pocket watches came in and was refused by a local merchant, young Sears saw an opportunity, contacted the manufacturer, and offered to sell the watches if he could keep any money above $12 per watch. Since the railroads had just adopted their own national time zone system in 1883, Sears reckoned all station agents and railroad men would need watches so he sold them for $14. (The U.S. government didn't adopt time zones until 1918.) Within six months he had made $5,000 and quit his job to start the R. W. Sears Watch Company in Minneapolis.

Sears began sending out flyers and placing ads in farm publications so farmers could keep up with "railroad time." He had quite a flare for writing copy and began to add additional items for sale. In 1887 he moved his business to Chicago and hired his first employee, a watch repairman named Alvah Roebuck, to repair any returned watches. Together they founded Sears, Roebuck & Company. (In 1895 Roebuck sold out to Sears for $20,000.) By 1897, Sears was mailing out a catalog of wares to more than 300,000 rural customers throughout the country that included farm implements, clothing, household goods, and even bicycles. In 1908, he added mail order home kits that included lumber, nails, shingles, indoor plumbing, wiring, central heating, and yes, even the kitchen sink (plus all other fixtures). Models cost from $360 to $2,890 and by the time kit home sales stopped in 1940, Sears, Roebuck & Company had sold more than 70,000 homes.

There are REITs that specialize in shopping centers and malls, commercial buildings, hospitals, residential housing, warehouses and other segments of the economy. And just like your other funds, you want no-load with low expense ratios.

Megatrends

Creative destruction is an ongoing process as new technologies and products make others obsolete. An inventor named An Wang developed a word-processing machine that made the typewriter obsolete. Then along came the PC which could do word-processing plus a whole lot more, and Wang Laboratories was gone. Things move so fast today that some industries will have a lifetime of a few years rather than decades. It would be nice to have a crystal ball to see the future, but that only happens in Disney movies, yet there are some trends that might portend great investing opportunities in the years ahead, so just for fun lets look at a few.

Cars – Trains, planes and automobiles have been working about the same way for the last hundred years, albeit with many improvements along the way. But now the ubiquitous automobile is undergoing profound change. Functions are being automated at an incredible rate, from auto parking to blind-spot warnings to autonomous breaking. Self-driving cars are being tested and eventually they will be totally autonomous without pedals or steering wheels, which brings up some questions.

Will that mean the end of tickets for speeding or DUI? Will insurance become dirt cheap if even needed? Since cars sit parked 90% of the time, wouldn't it make sense in urban areas to just have autonomous vehicles take us wherever we wanted to go and reduce the need for so many parking spaces? Would you even need to own one in the city, or have a second car in the burbs? Lyft and General Motors formed a $500 million partnership to develop a fleet of such vehicles and Uber inked a deal with Volvo to develop a fleet of robot cabs to roam the streets of Pittsburgh by 2021. And recently, Anheuser-Busch had a self-driving truck full of beer making deliveries in Fort Collins, Denver, and Colorado Springs. Do ya think some day someone might hack into one of those and hijack it?

Drones – Now that the FAA has published rules for drones, and the prices have fallen, their use is going to explode. Annual sales are projected to exceed $90 billion by 2025. Applications include agriculture, utilities, real estate, public safety, and even logistics.

More than 85% of Amazon deliveries weigh under five pounds.

IOT – The Internet of Things is coming. Controlling your thermostat and locking doors with your smart-phone doesn't even scratch the surface of what lies ahead. By 2020 half of the planet and 35 billion devices will be connected through the Internet. Sensors will eventually be everywhere and in everything, from biochips in farm animals to sensors in mechanical devices to report when service is needed and more. Some estimate it will be a $19 trillion market and require computer power to track 50 to 100 trillion objects at once. That's crazy.

Cybersecurity – With all this connectivity, security is going to be even bigger business. In the perpetual cat and mouse game of hacking, entire nations can be vulnerable.

Robotics – Just one Amazon warehouse has more than 3,000 Kiva robots moving about seamlessly, sorting through and delivering 3.5 million different products for shipment. More than 27,000 industrial robots worth $11 billion were shipped in the U.S. in 2014 and $16 billion in orders were placed in 2016. It's a big business and growing.

3-D printing – In 2014 they sent a 3-D printer up to the space station in case the astronauts needed to create a tool or a part. Then mechanical engineer Anjan Contractor won a $125,000 NASA grant to develop a 3-D printer to print a pizza, which he did. It took just a few minutes to print and 70 seconds to cook, and the ingredients have a shelf life of 30 years, ideal for space travel. Prosthetic joints have been printed, and now the FDA has given its approval for printing a drug, bringing closer the day when pharmacists will print custom designed medications for individuals.

They'll soon be a ubiquitous part of our culture, as common as the land-line of old, and the sky's the limit. Think about the impact 3-D printing will have on traditional manufacturing. If you need a crown, the dentist will print one for you. Need brake pads? The parts store will print one up in a jiffy. How about a pair of shoes, a lampshade or a hot dog, jet engine parts, or even body parts. It's a game changer. It's kind of like the replicator on Star Trek. Boggles the mind to ponder it!

Infrastructure – The 1930s to the 1960s were a heyday for infrastructure construction in the U.S. giving us the Golden Gate Bridge, Hoover Dam, Empire State Building, La Guardia Airport, the TVA, the interstate highway system, and thousands of post World War II projects as the country boomed. Now, a lot of that stuff is getting old.

Every four years the American Society of Civil Engineers issues a report card on the state of America's infrastructure. In the most recent (2013) report we improved to a D+, up from a D in 2009. Prior to 1980 we spent 3% of GDP on infrastructure, since then we spend about 2% while Europe spends 5% and China spends 9%. Transportation and water/sewer systems are the two worst areas, but we're also behind in maintenance and repair of levies, canals, ports, pipelines, subways, airports and the power grid. Sooner or later we're going to have to pay the piper. Therein lies opportunity.

Artificial Intelligence (AI) – Scientists claim that cheap parallel computation (huh?), an avalanche of data, and better algorithms in recent years have put us on the cusp of major breakthroughs in AI. Industry has spent $20 billion on AI research since 2009, and it's not just to play chess or Jeopardy or develop a self-driving car. Google is a huge player in the field. Within a decade or two, thinking machines will be able to translate any language for us or diagnose illness as well as or better than any doctor. Of course some smart folks like Stephen Hawking, Elon Musk and Bill Gates warn that AI taken too far could pose a threat to human survival. Oh joy! This used to be the stuff of sci-fi movies.

Millennials – When the vets returned after WWII they got married and created a baby boom. The huge number of Boomers drove the economy for decades, from the hospitals that birthed them, to the schools that educated them, to the job market that employed them. They needed toys and schoolbooks, cars and clothes, and their tastes and wants shaped the marketplace. The Millennials are now the demographic pig-in-the-python and will be setting trends and influencing the economy for a long time. Marketers are studying them ad nauseam to see what makes them tick and figure out what they like to wear, how they spend their leisure time, and what kind of workplace will best harness their skills.

World Population – Low or zero growth in the developed countries means an aging population, while the developing nations have high birth rates that will tax food and water supplies, and spark competition for resources. The population center of the planet is

---

A Killer App – Dan Bricklin was a student at the Harvard Business School in 1978 when he had an idea for a simple program for his hand-held calculator to help him analyze data for a class presentation. The professor and students were wowed, so Bricklin joined up with his friend Bob Frankston and formed a company called Software Arts (later VisiCorp) to market it. They considered calling the software Compulator, Calculedger, or Electroledger but settled on the name VisiCalc and it soon became an integral part of the newly released Apple II personal computer. Soon after, Lotus and Microsoft came out with competing programs and by 1984 VisiCorp was insolvent and acquired by Lotus. Today it's a ubiquitous part of business culture that we know simply as a spreadsheet. Steve Jobs said VisiCalc is what allowed Apple to be successful, and in the "Bricklin Classroom" at Harvard where he conceived the idea, is a plaque to commemorate "the original killer app of the information age."

shifting to Asia where they are building like crazy to meet the needs of their people. In China alone, they poured more concrete in three years (2011-2013) than America poured in the last century (1901-2000). This shift will create a lot of turmoil but also opportunity. Think global.

The Bottom Line

You did it! You got through the toughest part of the book and maintained your sanity, I hope. I knew you could. Now, after a one page recap, go treat yourself to a root beer.

To use a baseball analogy, successful long term investing is all about "small ball." It's not about swinging for the fences and hitting a home run now and then, with a lot of strikeouts in between, but rather making steady progress by hitting singles and doubles. I'm afraid it's rather mundane and actually boring, but over time will pay big dividends (pun intended). Over the years I'm sure you're going to encounter friends or acquaintances telling you about the "killing" they made in this or that scheme or investment, but be content with the course you've set and remember, you're in this for the long run.
So what have we learned so far?

- Market risk decreases with longer time periods—there's never been a loss investing in the stock market over a 20 year period.
- A couple of Nobel laureates told us asset allocation (the percentage of stocks, bonds and cash) is the biggest determinate of portfolio performance.
- Another Nobel laureate said that our emotions (fear and greed) play a big role in financial decision-making.
- Mutual funds allow small investors to buy into a diversified, professionally managed investment portfolio that they otherwise might not be able to afford or be capable of managing.
- No-load mutual fund companies have no sales commissions.
- Fees have the biggest impact on a mutual fund's performance.
- Index funds and ETFs have the lowest fees.
- You need to determine your tolerance for risk to help plan asset allocation.
- Target funds have the least hassle. If you hate investing, this is your puppy.
- Index funds have the lowest expenses but require a little work.
- Actively managed funds cost more and require more work.
- If you want to invest in individual stocks, work with a professional.

*© 2016 Morningstar, Inc. All Rights Reserved. The information contained herein: (1) is proprietary to Morningstar and/or its content providers; (2) may not be copied or distributed; (3) does not constitute investment advice offered by Morningstar; and (4) is not warranted to be accurate, complete or timely. Neither Morningstar nor its content providers are responsible for any damages or losses arising from any use of this information. Past performance is no guarantee of future results. Use of information from Morningstar does not necessarily constitute agreement by Morningstar, Inc. of any investment philosophy or strategy presented in this publication.

Part III

Spending

"The cornerstone of democracy rests on the
foundation of an educated electorate."
Thomas Jefferson

"Money is like manure. If you spread it around, it does a lot of good,
but if you pile it up in one place it stinks like hell."
Clint Murchison
Founder of the Dallas Cowboys

"I'm not opposed to making money, believe me. But I think the
only reason to have money is to do some good with it."
Joe Paterno
Football coach

"There's nothing wrong with money.
Money is good if you spend it wisely and give it away."
Truett Cathy
Founder Chic-fil-A

"I gave my daughter an unlimited budget, and she exceeded it."
Nick Saban
Football coach
Discussing his daughter's wedding

"Some people wanted champagne and caviar
when they should have had beer and hot dogs."
Dwight D Eisenhower

"24 hours in a day and 24 beers in a case.
Coincidence? I think not."
H. L. Mencken
Writer

The Big Picture

This section is about how spending can lead to debt if you're not careful, and how to deal with debt if you've already accumulated some. Millennials are now the alpha-influencers in the marketplace so we'll look at spending for big ticket items like houses, cars, weddings and education. We'll also delve into delayed gratification, the value of education, credit reports and scores, insurance, and even retirement spending.

When we shop, whether for a pair of shoes, a car or a house, most of us tend to buy based on emotion, then justify it with logic. Like those in Generation X ahead of them, a lot of older Millennials grew up in an age of easy credit and even easier spending, so it should come as no surprise that debt is a major player in their lives. What's more, the single largest debt most Millennials have accumulated is student loans. So we'll spend quite a bit of time dealing with education and you'll see that with some self-discipline and budgeting you can get out from under this load. Younger Millennials who are not yet in college can avoid a similar situation by being smart about their education decisions.

Windfalls

Like sauerkraut ice cream, some things just don't go well together, and when people with poor financial literacy and discipline receive a large sum of money, they often end up with a bad taste in their mouth. Sudden wealth doesn't build character; it just magnifies all the good and bad traits of the newly rich.

Rick, Cryder and Lowenstein, the researchers you met in Part I, concluded that about 16% of us seem to be hard-wired to being spendthrifts. But when it comes to windfalls, many more of us seem to have brain-farts of epic proportions as we realize we can now spend beyond our norm.

Homer Simpson's neighbor Maude Flanders died at the hands of a tee-shirt cannoneer at the Springfield Speedway. (Ned and the boys still mourn her passing.) The odds of that happening are a gizillion to one, but it did. The odds of winning big bucks in the lottery are pretty long too, but it happens, and when it does it's not always for the better. For many lottery winners the initial reaction is to spend, spend, spend, and even quit their jobs.

Researchers at the University of Pittsburgh, Vanderbilt University and the University of

Kentucky studied lottery winners and discovered that they file for bankruptcy at more than twice the rate of the population as a whole. Their study looked at winners of $50,000 to $150,000 in the Florida Fantasy Five game. The conclusion was that the typical winner had below average income, education and financial literacy and treated their winnings much less cautiously than their paychecks. Even though the average winnings were more than the average debt of the winners, they spent most of the cash instead of paying off debt, elevated their lifestyle to unsustainable levels and started down a road to ruin.

Professional athletes are even worse than lottery winners. Though they typically have short careers, as a group, pro athletes earn a very good wage while playing. Consider the following average salaries, career length, and career earnings for pro athletes:

    Basketball (NBA) $5.15 million; 4.8 years; $24.7 million
    Baseball (MLB) $3.2 million; 5.6 years; $17.9 million
    Hockey (NHL) $2.4 million; 5.5 years; $13.2 million
    Football (NFL) $1.9 million; 3.5 years; $6.7 million

A Sports Illustrated story and the ESPN documentary "Broke" reported that 78% of NFL players were broke three years after retirement, and 60% of NBA players were broke five years after leaving the game. Antoine Walker retired in 2006 after playing 13 years in the NBA and earning more than $100 million. He filed for bankruptcy in 2010 claiming assets of $4.3 million and debts of $12.7 million. Why do young, newly rich individuals allow their fortunes to slip away so quickly? Mostly it's because of limited financial literacy; the belief that the money would last forever; the need to keep up with their peers with all the bling, the entourage, and the wheels; underestimating taxes; and getting poor financial advice from unscrupulous agents, accountants and friends.

Blowing a windfall is not the exclusive purview of lotto winners and jocks however. So listen up Millennials: I have some good news for you, if not for me. Over the next three decades you and the GenX gang stand to inherit about $30 trillion (that's trillion, with a T) in the largest transfer of wealth in the history of planet earth, due to the pending die-off of the Boomers. That's a lot of money. Now listen up again Millennials, I have some bad news for you: Statistics show that 70% of you will blow the inheritance. But don't fret—if you don't spend it, your children likely will finish the job, because the same stats show that by the third generation, 90% of families will have squandered the family assets.

These numbers play out throughout the industrial world, not just here in the U.S. It's funny, but the values that allowed first generation creators of wealth to amass their money—hard work, self-discipline and perseverance—aren't necessarily adopted by the second generation, because many parents want their children to have a better life than they did and give the kids what the parents themselves missed out on. Plus there's a reluctance to talk about family finances and handling money within most families. Unfortunately, though parents want to provide some security for their children and grandchildren, their failure to teach their kids the values needed to hang on to a buck usually means the family assets are lost. Warren Buffett, who is leaving 99% of his wealth to charity, said it best. He's not cutting his children out of his will, but said he will leave them "enough money so that they would feel they could do anything, but not so much that they could do nothing." There's a wise man.

Door to Door – Bill Porter was born in San Francisco in 1932 with a severe case of cerebral palsy. His family moved to Portland, Oregon, when he was young, and though he was only able to walk and talk with considerable difficulty and had the use of but one hand, he finished high school. After graduation he was told by the state that he was unemployable and was offered disability, however Bill refused and applied to the Fuller Brush Company for a door to door sales job. He was turned down.

Undeterred, he applied to the J.R. Watkins Company, a purveyor of household goods and personnel care products, for a commission only sales position and was again turned down, but this time Bill dug in his heels and convinced them to give him a crack at the worst territory they had. Unable to drive, he would take a bus and then walk eight to ten miles every day, carrying a suitcase with pictures of his products, since the real products would have been too heavy for him to carry. Little by little orders started to come in, which his mother would deliver when the products arrived, and after a while he was the top salesman in Portland, then the west coast, and eventually the entire country. He gained fame in 1995, when the local newspaper ran a story about his dogged determination, and was eventually featured in Reader's Digest, ABC's 20/20 and in an Emmy-winning made-for-TV movie staring William H. Macy and Helen Mirren. Mr. Porter died in December 2013 at age 81 having shown the world that with perseverance, anything is possible.

Debt

You know why it's important to save and how to invest, but what if you're you're so buried in debt from your spendthrift days that you can't come up with a spare nickel, let alone pay your bills and save 15% for retirement. Life happens, and with the average consumer debt at $29,000 some people end up in this situation. It's no use looking back and moaning about it or burying your head in the sand. You need to look forward and make a plan or you'll stay where you are and suffer. First you have to get an idea of just how deep a hole you've put yourself in and see if it's possible to get out. In most cases the problem is solvable and the solution is simple, but the discipline to see it through can be tough. The problem usually is that you have an imbalance in your balance sheet—not enough coming in and too much going out—so you'll need to follow a few Do's and Don'ts to get this debt monkey off your back. For a while it might mean the end of life as you know it and you'll need to tell your friends you'll be a social no-show for the foreseeable future. And be aware, you might get some push-back from a few of your friends, especially those in a similar position. So here are some suggestions:

DO

* Work more. If you can't get overtime, get a second or even a third job. Buy and sell on Ebay.
* Find a cheaper place to live. Roommates are good – learn to like them. Move back in with your parents if you need to. (OMG! Can't believe I said that.)
* Get rid of the bundle with 300 channels and a phone that does everything. Flip phones still work, and Netflix, Hulu, or Roku type services are cheap.
* If you have a car payment, lower it or make it go away by trading down. Buses and subways are your friend and walking is good for your health.
* Take lunch to work, every day.
* Dump the health club membership. Push-ups at home and walking will have to work for now.
* Exist on a cash only basis with debit cards or greenbacks and use only cash for purchases under $20. You may need to cut up your credit cards (plastic surgery)
* Live like a Trappist monk or nun (except for the beer brewing part). Austerity is your middle name.
* Be creative in finding ways to make more money and spend less.

DON'T

* Go to happy hour on Friday night — you're too busy delivering pizza (your second job).
* Go tailgating and partying with friends on the weekend — you're too busy mowing lawns, or working at the shoe store, or waiting tables (your third job).
* Eat out 'til the first credit card is paid off. Peanut butter, rice and beans are your new steak.

Here's the plan. Let's say that before you became a believer in thrift and saving, you amassed more than $32,000 in credit card debt that you're trying to get out from under. Just making the minimum payment is costing almost a grand a month, but now that you're working a second job, living like a monk and have no social life, you do have an extra $525 to put toward the debt. If you want to know how best to attack this, any CPA, bean-counter, or even eighth grade math teacher will tell you the most efficient way is to throw the extra money at the highest interest rate card first, since that's the one that's costing you the most money. In the following example it means sending the extra $525 to Visa 1 every month, which makes perfect mathematical sense.

But there's another school of thought when it comes to paying down debt. Several studies show that paying off the smallest debt first, regardless of interest rate, is more likely to lead to success. It's kind of like dieting. If you don't see any results early on, you become discouraged and fall off the wagon.

Card	Amount	Interest	Minimum
Visa 1	$12,000	24%	$360
Visa 2	$ 6,600	19%	$198
Visa 3	$ 5,200	22%	$156
MasterCard 1	$ 4,200	17%	$126
MasterCard 2	$ 1,900	19%	$ 57
Target	$ 1,400	12%	$ 42
Kohl's	$ 900	13%	$ 27
Total	$32,200		$966

A better way to attack this is to send the extra $525 to Kohl's, and in two months it's gone. Besides getting a big psychological boost, you get to celebrate with dinner out and perhaps a root beer, or even a Trappist brew. One down, six to go. Next, focus on the Target bill, except now you're sending $552 each month ($525 plus the $27 you were sending to Kohl's). In three months Target is paid off, and you're throwing $594 a month ($525+$27+$42) at MasterCard 2. In about three months that's done, too — three down, four to go — and you go after MasterCard 1. This snowball effect has you increasing the monthly payment with every card you pay off, so when you get to the last one you're like a runner finishing a marathon, endorphins racing through your brain and the end in sight as you attack the big nut — the $12,000 Visa 1 bill — with $1,131 every month. Wow! I knew you could do it.

But there are times when it might be more difficult if not impossible to work your way out of a hole. To get a feel for what you face, you need to determine your debt ratio, which is your gross monthly income divided by your total monthly debt payments. Debt payments in this case are your rent/mortgage, car loan, insurance, credit card, student loan and any other payments you're obligated to make. Follow these ballpark guidelines to determine if you can do it or if you're going to need help.

* **Below 40%** is acceptable and means you have your spending under control;
* **40% to 54%** could portend financial difficulties and you need to work on reducing the debt burden;
* **55% and above** means you're in over your head and need professional help.

If you can't seem to work and save your way out of debt and are falling further behind, the first thing you need to do is contact your lenders and credit card companies and let them know. Don't ignore it in hopes it will go away. Most of them will work directly with you because it's in their best interest to eventually get paid rather than having to write off the debt and take a loss. If you're so buried that you need professional help, there are two general ways to go, a debt settlement company or credit counseling service.

Debt Settlement Companies: Beware when dealing with these guys. Sometimes called Credit Repair Companies, they are for-profit organizations that offer to arrange settlements with your creditors. They often tell you to stop making payments so the debt goes to a collection agency, then settle for a lump sum payment for something less than the full amount. They charge hefty fees and often skirt or disregard the law. For instance, the FTCs Telemarketing Sales Rule prohibits telemarketers from charging a fee until the debt is settled, reduced, or the terms of the debt are changed. But there is an exemption if clients have a face-to-face meeting, so some companies send a "representative" for you to "sign" some papers, which allows them to circumvent the restriction on up-front fees. Other debt settlement companies simply ignore the law altogether and demand payment in advance, which of course is illegal. Contrary to what most of these companies advertise, there are no guaranteed up-front agreements as to how much of the debt you'll end up paying, and they usually don't get terms any better than if you were to talk to the creditors or debt collectors yourself. There are better options.

Credit Counseling Organizations: These are community based, non-profit agencies that offer free and confidential financial counseling. The best way to find one is to go to the National Foundation for Credit Counseling website at **nfcc.org**. NFCC member agencies offer free financial education and debt, student loan, mortgage, and bankruptcy counseling in addition to debt management plans. In their debt management plans, for which they do charge a small monthly fee, they do not reduce the amount you owe by forcing the debt into collections. They usually can lower your monthly payment by reaching up-front agreements with creditors to reduce interest rates and waive late fees. Even if you don't enter a debt management program, credit counseling agencies can provide good professional advice regarding many money problems.

Not All Debt is Created Equal

If you take out a mortgage on a home, your loan is secured by the house, and if you don't pay on time the bank can foreclose on the debt and take your home. Same thing for a car loan — if you don't pay, they're going to repo your wheels. But credit card debt is unsecured, meaning if you don't pay you have no hard assets directly at risk. That's not to say there's no down side and you needn't worry about paying your credit cards.

Here's how it works out if you fail to pay your credit card or unsecured debt. After a while, the credit card company usually sells the debt to a collection agency at less than face value and gets it off their books. The collection company, which now owns the debt, contacts you to work out an arrangement with the goal of getting as much money as possible as quickly as possible; they're not interested in getting ten bucks a month for the rest of your life. You can usually negotiate with them and the amount they will settle for is based on their perception of your ability to pay. If you're 99 years old, without a job, living on social

---

Phone Me – In case you were wondering, spoken language has been around for more than 100,000 years. Linguists tell us there are around 7,000 languages in the world today of which about 500 are nearly extinct. Languages are made up of phonemes, which are units of sound that allow us to distinguish one word from another. Xoo, spoken in the Kalahari Desert of Botswana has the most phonemes with 112 and Rotokas, of Papua New Guinea has but 11. English has 44. While English has more words than any other language with more than one million, we don't have the largest alphabet. That honor goes to Khmer with 74 letters while Rotokas has only 12, with six consonants and six vowels.

In the 1880s, Dr. Ludwik Zamenh of Poland thought this was all a bit much and constructed an easy to learn, universal second language – everyone was to keep their native tongue - called Esperanto to foster peace and understanding among nations. In 1910 he was nominated for the Nobel Peace Prize for his efforts. About 2,000,000 people speak Esperanto today and, with more than 225,000 articles on Wikipedia, it's the 32nd largest contributor.

security, and don't have a bank account or own your home, or even a car, you're pretty much untouchable, and they will get nothing. But if you just won the lottery, or own a home, or have a good job, the collection agency will want one hundred cents on the dollar and will come after you. (Of course if you do have a good paying job you should pay your legitimate debts.)

Either way your credit is ruined, but if you're 99 years old, who cares? If you're not, you can start down a slippery slope that leads to ruin. Should you not reach agreement with the collection agency, they can go to court and get a judgment against you and then go back to court with judgment in hand, and ask the judge for a lien against your property or a garnishment of your wages.

When it comes to debt, people oftentimes develop a "bunker mentality" and bury their heads in the sand in hopes the problem will go away, but it rarely does. So if you have debt of any kind, it behooves you to work toward resolving it.

Here's an example of what not to do when it comes to credit card debt. I once spoke with a woman who, two years earlier, had amassed $30,000 in credit card debt and took out a home equity line of credit (HELOC) to pay it off, which means she had securitized the debt and put her home at risk. When I spoke with

A Really Bad Idea.

> **Bunkers** – The threat of nuclear war during the Cold War was very real, and the government took steps to provide for continuity of operations should the worst happen. Nestled in the Allegheny Mountains near White Sulphur Springs, WV, is the iconic Greenbriar Hotel luxury resort with five golf courses, swimming pools, horse stables and a casino. But beneath the Greenbriar lies a secret bunker, constructed in the 1950s, to house the Congress of the United States plus their staff (up to 1,100 people) so they could continue operating. In 1992 the Greenbriar gave up its secret when its existence was revealed in a Washington Post article. Among numerous other bunkers surrounding our nation's capital is one buried deep in Mount Weather, VA, to house all the Executive Branch departments and agencies (which was activated for the first time after the 911 attack); another inside Raven Rock Mountain, PA with facilities for the Pentagon; and one in Mount Pony, VA, constructed to house the Federal Reserve. I suspect they all have an ample supply of beer.

her, she had accumulated an additional $18,000 on her cards and now had debt collectors after her and was struggling to make her HELOC payment. She had simply rearranged the deck chairs on the Titanic, putting off for a short time her inevitable fate, and like a lot of people, had focused on the symptom and not the illness. She was a spendthrift, had no self-discipline, and was in need of plastic surgery. The lesson here is to get control of your debt and never turn unsecured debt into secured debt.

The 800-Pound Gorilla

Just like other generations, the biggest purchase most Millennials will make is a home. There is currently more than $13 trillion dollars of outstanding mortgage debt in the U.S. Granted that's a lot of money, but mortgage lenders protect themselves by establishing lending guidelines for anyone who wants to borrow money to buy a house, plus as we just learned, mortgage debt is secured by the property. The maximum amount of a loan is based on your ability to repay the debt. Makes sense, doesn't it? Generally speaking, after you've submitted pay stubs, tax returns, W-2 forms, bank statements and other documents, the lender verifies that the borrower's total recurring debts (that includes student loans) do not exceed more than 43% of gross income, and that the mortgage payment itself (including taxes and insurance) does not exceed 28% of gross monthly income. Beginning around the turn of the century, for a bunch of different reasons, the mortgage industry ignored its own lending guidelines and in 2007 the house of cards this created came crashing down, causing chaos that rippled around the world.

The next largest purchase for most Millennials will be an education. We Americans now have $1.25 trillion in outstanding student debt, and as brainsick as it may sound, unlike mortgages, the maximum amount one can borrow is not based on the borrower's ability to repay. Someone working toward a degree in penguin studies can borrow as much as someone majoring in electrical engineering. Federal loans can go in excess of $50,000 for an undergraduate degree, and if you throw in private student loans, the total debt can easily reach six figures. So, if you go to Prestige U. and major in Beer Pong, you may find yourself paying on student debt for the next twenty-five years. When it comes to borrowing, a good rule of thumb is that your student debt should not exceed the expected first year annual earnings in the field in which you're getting a degree. Check out the Bureau of Labor Statistics website (**bls.gov**) and find salary information on hundreds of occupations.

Since a college education is one of the largest and most important investments a person can make, it's important to approach the decision with eyes wide open and get as much information as possible. In 2013 a bi-partisan bill called *The Student Right to Know Before You Go Act* was introduced in Congress which would have required colleges and universities to provide prospective students with information on average student debt, plus the median annual earnings for various degrees two, six and 15 years after graduating. Unfortunately the bill was not enacted. Your ability to repay needs to be a consideration when taking on student debt, and if the government and banks won't do it, you'll need to do it yourself.

Theremin – Do you remember the wavy, almost eerie sounds in that Beach Boys oldie "Good Vibrations"? We can thank Léon Theremin for that. He was a Russian scientist, and in 1920 invented an electronic musical instrument that was played without the performer touching the instrument. Referred to as a theremin (sometimes called a etherphone or thereminophone) it had two antennas, one vertical for pitch and one horizontal for volume, that produced sound when the performer's hands were moved in proximity to the antennas. After touring Europe in 1927, he came to the United States, where he patented his invention and sold the manufacturing rights to RCA. Theremin played at Carnegie Hall and with the New York Philharmonic, and while working with the American Negro Ballet married a dancer named Lavinia Williams. Because it was a mixed race marriage they were ostracized in the music and scientific communities, and by 1938 were in deep financial difficulty. One step ahead of the IRS, Theremin abruptly abandoned his wife and returned to the Soviet Union, where he was quickly thrown into the gulag for being a capitalist.

That's when things got interesting. Recognizing his talents, the secret police put Theremin to work in the prison laboratory where he developed a revolutionary listening device that became known as "The Thing." The KGB hid one in a carved wooden copy of the Great Seal of the United States that was presented to U.S. Ambassador Averell Harriman by a group of schoolchildren in 1945. "The Thing" allowed the KGB to listen in on all conversations in the ambassador's residence until accidentally being discovered seven years later. Léon Theremin died a Soviet hero in 1993 at age 97, but his musical creation lives on in the music of Led Zeppelin, the Beach Boys and the Rolling Stones, plus numerous movies and television shows.

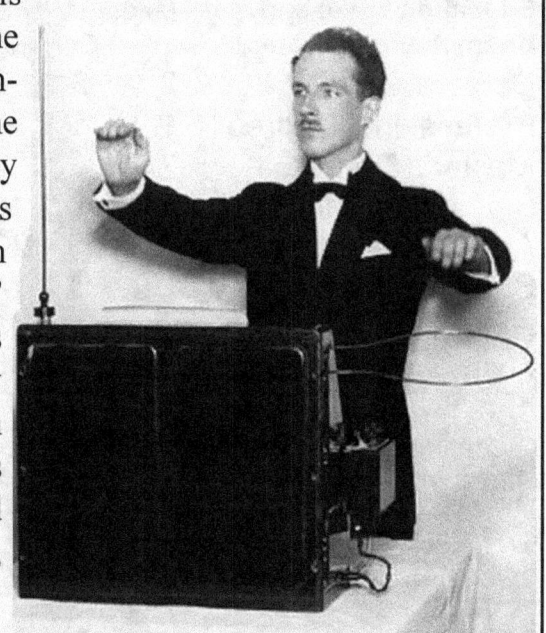

This makes picking the right school important. PayScale, Inc. put out a college return-on-investment report (**payscale.com/college-roi**) that shows the difference between the 20 year median pay for graduates with bachelor's degrees and the 24 year pay for high school graduates at more than a thousand colleges and universities. It's organized by schools, not majors, and shows that sometimes a college degree can have a negative ROI. For example, a graduate of Fayetteville State University, where the total cost of a four year education is only $53,100 but has a 32% graduation rate and typically takes five years to finish, can expect to earn $62,100 less than a high school graduate over the next 20 years. Compare that to top ranked Harvey Mudd College where it costs $237,700 for a bachelor's degree, but has a 91% graduation rate in four years, and the typical grad can expect to earn $985,300 more than a high school counterpart. Which is the better deal? Granted, a negative ROI is a rarity, and I don't want to disparage Fayetteville State, but in purely business terms, some schools are just better investments.

A note to the parents of Millennials. If you thought about tapping your 401k or IRA to pay for your child's education, DON'T DO IT! It's an honorable thought, and I know you mean well, but remember, you can borrow for education, but you can't borrow for retirement. A better idea is to help your child pay off student loans after graduation to whatever degree you're able.

Investing In Yourself

Improving oneself is always a good idea, and the burden of student loans should not be a reason to skip higher education, but you have to be smart about how you go about it. Without a doubt, if you choose the right school and field of study, investing in an education is a good deal. In 1973, more than 70% of jobs required only a high school diploma, but today a person with a high school diploma is competitive for only about one-third of jobs, and that number is declining rapidly. Take a look at this information put out by the Bureau of Labor Statistics with data from 2014.

Education Level and Unemployment Rate		Median Weekly Earnings
Doctoral Degree	2.1	$ 1,591
Professional Degree	1.9	$ 1,639
Master's Degree	2.8	$ 1,326
Bachelor's Degree	3.5	$ 1,101
Associate Degree	4.5	$ 792
Some College	6	$ 741
High School Diploma	6	$ 488
Less Than High School	9	$ 488

So if one were to ask the question, "What's a sheepskin worth?" it seems clear to deduce from this data that education has value. It clearly shows that the higher the degree, the higher the income, and studies have shown that on average, college graduates earn about one million dollars more than high school graduates over their lifetime.

But as we know, there are all kinds of schools and all kinds of degrees, and with education costs rising so fast, you need to decide if it's worth the investment, and give some thought to how you'll pay for it. If you spend five years getting a degree in something-or-other-studies and finish owing $80,000 in loans, was it the smart thing to do? Can you pay that debt?

To further depress you, know that Americans pay seven times what students in other industrial nations pay, partly because only 40% of our students graduate in four years and 60% in six years, partly because our education costs have gone bonkers, and partly because many kids go to college just to soak up the "college experience" without any goals or idea of what they want to do in life. Not knowing what area of study you want to pursue in college is not unusual and many students graduate and still have no idea what field they want to work in, but you don't want to go broke figuring it out.

STEM

The big buzzword in education and the business world these days is STEM, meaning science, technology, engineering and math. For better or worse, STEM, along with business, is where the money is today. People with STEM degrees are the ones who design, build and repair things, solve problems, and create value, and society puts a premium on that. STEM and business majors are in demand out of college, are offered the highest salaries, and now account for almost half of college graduates. But does this mean everyone should be a STEMster? I don't think so. Lord knows we need counselors to help us deal with life's troubles, entertainers to make us laugh and cry, social workers to help the less fortunate, theologians to give us guidance, and artists for art's sake. We also need plumbers,

Skins – Over the millennia, as we progressed from writing on clay tablets, to papyrus, and then paper, we were also writing on skins. In a process called liming, the skins of sheep and goats were soaked in an alkali solution and then scraped, stretched and dried to create parchment. (When calfskin was used, it was usually referred to as vellum.) If the skins were soaked in an acid solution it was called tanning and they became leather. Parchment was highly prized for its durability and was used for luxury manuscripts, government documents and diplomas. Two of the last American schools to offer real sheepskin diplomas, Notre Dame and Rice University, discontinued them in 2012.

carpenters, and electricians to build and repair houses, mechanics to fix our cars, farmers to feed us, teachers to educate us, bureaucrats to keep the trolly on the tracks and even philosophers to ponder the meaning of life. Those who enjoy what they do are better and happier people and more productive workers, and I personally believe you're better off finding your passion, as long as that passion allows you to earn a living. So be smart about how you get your degree, and go for it.

Peter Cappelli of the Wharton School of Business wrote a book called ***Will College Pay Off? A Guide to the Most Important Financial Decision You'll Ever Make*** and argues that STEM might not be as great as some think it is. His research shows that science and math majors with bachelor's degrees earn about the same as sociology majors. Engineers get the highest paying jobs after graduation, but there's a good bit of risk involved because engineering is so very specific—an electrical engineer can't do the job of a civil engineer for example—and market needs change over time. Ten years ago petroleum engineers had a tough time finding work, then fracking came along and demand and salaries skyrocketed, but crude prices have fallen a lot lately, and if they stay low for a prolonged period of time, the hoard of newly minted petroleum engineers might find a tough job market again. And in the IT world there are plenty of jobs, but there often isn't much upward mobility which produces a lot of turnover.

So to answer Professor Cappelli's question—Will college pay off?—the answer is: It depends. With costs and borrowing at an all-time high, and such low graduation rates, college might not be the best place for a lot of Millennials right out of high school. More students are taking a gap year (like Malia Obama) to think about what they want to do with their lives or to earn some money. Why go into debt for something you may not enjoy or finish? Finishing what you start is important. High school graduates do better in the job market than those with GEDs because a diploma shows they were able to finish the task at hand, and it's the same with college.

Many students just are not into academics and would rather work with their hands, and there's nothing wrong with that. Skilled craftsmen are in short supply in a lot of fields, and you can take some vocational school courses concurrently with high school and get into the workforce a lot sooner than the academic types. As Bubbette showed us, the disciplined early saver can win the race.

Cappelli also says a bachelor's degree alone no longer guarantees a good career and that what you do during college is just as important as the classes you take. Many employers care more about work experiences, internships, extracurricular activities and experience than academics. They want to know that you can work with other people and think critically, and they're looking for good verbal and written communication skills and no, texting doesn't count. He suggests taking a variety of courses and selecting as broad a major as possible. A narrowly focused major like turf engineering, pharmaceutical sales or international tourism (actual majors) may have been big when you started school, but four or five years later when you graduate, it might not do much for you if those markets are down. Of course, Cappelli is a Wharton bean-counter and doesn't delve much into the fact that attending college, even for underwater basket weaving, usually makes you a more well-rounded individual, and that's good for society, but even so, I think I'm siding with the professor on this one.

So what's the best way to approach this college thing? If money is of no concern, go to whatever school suits your needs and desires, but if you want to maximize your educational investment and minimize your debt, do your homework. Don't select a school because you like their football team, or that's where all your friends are going, or you want to be closer to the beach. Follow the path that gives you the biggest bang for your buck. You can just about get an Ivy League education at Podunk State if you're a hard-working, dedicated student.

Let's say you're crazy about penguins and want to get a PhD in penguinology (I know, but it's all I could think of) and make it your life's work. Here's the plan: First two years, or all four if they have a biology degree program, are at the local community college while you work nights and live at home. Summer internships at any zoo or aquarium that has penguins while you deliver pizzas on weekends, followed by a graduate assistant position in ornithology at Podunk State. Then, because of all the articles you submitted to the ***Birdwatcher's Journal*** and your stellar grades, you get a National Science Foundation fellowship in Antarctica to do research for your dissertation, where you discover the tracks made by Emperor penguins on their trek from the sea to the breeding colony exactly match the Nazca geoglyphs in southern Peru. Now you're a rock star throughout the bird watching world and have job offers from all over the southern hemisphere. Sorry, got carried away. Maybe you just get to winter over in Antarctica, but at least you're debt free.

While many STEMsters with bachelor degrees start out with bigger paychecks, it's sometimes those in other fields who get the biggest bang for their buck when it comes to graduate school. If the aforementioned petroleum engineer invests in an advanced degree, he or she can expect very little bump in earnings according to research from Georgetown University, but those majoring in humanities, liberal arts, social work, education, business, public policy and agriculture earn about 33% more than their counterparts with bachelor degrees, making it well worth the effort. The biggest payoff, according to the research, was for biology and life sciences majors, with a 63% increase in earnings.

Grad school student debt now averages more than $57,000 but what's even more shocking is that 25% of students borrow $100,000 or more, and 10% borrow $150,000 or more. OMG! I hope they're all in medical school. If you're thinking of taking the plunge and going for an advanced degree, ask yourself this: Is my graduate degree worth the cost? It usually is, provided you don't break the bank doing it, so look before you leap.

> **Extreme Solutions** – Ken Ilgunas graduated with $32,000 in student loan debt and moved to Alaska to be a tour guide and work odd jobs, one of which was transporting "voyagers" (people who dress up like 18th century fur traders) across Ontario, Canada, in a canoe. Not a lot of places to blow money in the wilderness, and he paid the debt off in just over two years. He then headed to grad school where he lived in his van, and went on to write a book about it called *Walden on Wheels: On The Open Road From Debt to Freedom*.
>
>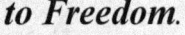
>
> Holly Morganelli paid off $60,000 in student loans by moving to Buenos Aries to teach English, and then Qatar, where she found a job as a librarian. Her room and board in Qatar was paid for, and since she was out of the country, her income was exempt from U.S. taxes. She was debt free in less than two years.
>
> In 2008, Natalie Dylan reportedly partnered with the Moonlight Bunny Ranch, a legal brothel in Nevada, to auction off her virginity to pay off $100,000 in student loans, which she claimed were fraudulently taken out by her step-father. The winning bid came in at $1 million. Some say it was just a publicity stunt, but either way, she gets points for creativity.

FAFSA

If you decide that higher education is for you but you can't cover the cost, even attending Podunk U. while living at home, then you're going to have to enter the murky world of student loans. Generally you can borrow for education from two sources, a federal loan directly from the Department of Education, or a private bank loan, like those offered by SLM Corporation, commonly known as Sallie Mae. Federal loans have fixed interest rates, flexible repayment options and even loan forgiveness in some cases, but most private loans have variable interest rates which can increase over time and few if any payment options. So it makes sense to always try for federal dollars first.

The process begins with the FAFSA, the Free Application for Federal Student Aid, created by the U.S. Department of Education. You should fill one out even if you think you're not eligible for any financial aid. (Last year $2.9 billion in Federal grant money went unclaimed for lack of a FAFSA.) Once you complete the form you'll receive a Student Aid Report which has all the info you submitted on the FASFA, so you can check or modify it, plus your Expected Family Contribution (EFC). The schools you apply to will subtract the EFC from the Cost of Attendance (COA) to determine your Financial Need based on your major, where you live, your year in school or GPA, among other things.

COA – EFC = FINANCIAL NEED

The thing to keep in mind is that the school, not the Federal government, determines your financial need and then the amount of aid you will receive. If you applied to three different schools that all had the same COA, the financial need would be about the same at all three, but the financial aid offered could differ substantially. That's because each school has its own metric. One might give preference to blue-eyed Irish girls wearing glasses while another might lean toward left-handed Aborigines who have trained a wild Dingo. Just kidding. It's not quite that crazy, but schools do give increased weight to applicants based on your majors, where you live, your year in school, or your GPA.

Once the need-based aid is established, the school will determine your non-need-based aid by subtracting the aid awarded so far from the COA. (The EFC is not used to compute non-need-based aid.) Again, each school has its own metric.

Unless you do a little digging, you may not know how much aid you're going to receive until you've applied and been accepted to a school. To get an estimate of how much aid you might be awarded, look for the school's *net price calculator* on their website. This shows you how much students similar to you paid to attend the previous year. Then you can look at things like graduation rates, average debt at graduation, and the average need-based and non-need-based aid met to get a better feel for what it's going to cost you. To find all this data spend some time snooping around the following websites:

* College Affordability and Transparency Center at **collegecost.ed.gov**
* National Center for Educational Statistics at **nces.ed.gov/ipeds**
* Kiplinger's Personal Finance at **kiplinger.com** (search for "Best College Values")

Of the roughly twenty million students attending college, about twelve million borrow money to cover the costs, but you need to be smart about how you go about it. Here's the order in which you should seek education money:

Pell Grants – Unlike loans, grants do not have to be repaid. Pell grants are need-based and for full-time undergraduate students only. The max amount is $5,815 per 12 month period from 1 July to 30 June, but the actual amount you get is based on your EFC and the cost of attendance.

Perkins Loans – Available for students with exceptional financial need in undergraduate and graduate courses of study. Not all schools participate, and funds are limited so apply early. Annual max of $5,500 with a cap of $27,500 for undergraduate. Repayment begins nine months after leaving school.

Direct Subsidized Loans – Called called Stafford Loans until 2011, these are need-based loans available to undergraduate students. The interest on the loan is paid by the government while you are in school and for six months after leaving school. The max amount you can borrow is $3,500 the first year, $4,500 the second year, $5,500 for the third and subsequent years, with a maximum total of $23,000. Your school determines how much you can borrow.

Direct Unsubsidized Loans – These are non-need-based loans available to both undergraduate and graduate students. Interest accumulates from day one and is added to the principle. Your school determines how much you can borrow, and there is a $31,000 total maximum, which also includes any Direct Subsidized Loans. If you are 24 years old, married, or a veteran, you are considered an "independent" student and different rules and dollar limits apply.

Federal Work Study – A needs-based program that provides part-time employment in community service, or when possible, work related to your course of study.

State Financial Aid – Every state offers aid to some degree. See **finaid.org/otheraid** or talk to the financial aid office.

Institutional Scholarships – for those who excel in academics, athletics, performing arts, etc.

Outside Aid – There are hundreds of random scholarships based on religion, ethnicity, college major, sexual orientation, family history, medical condition and a host of other things. (**fastweb.com**, **bigfuture.collegeboard.org**, **careeronestop.org/scholarshipfinder**, are good websites to search)

Private Bank Student Loans – This is your loan of last resort. There are two basic types of private bank loans: school-channel loans, and direct-to-consumer loans. School-channel loans are "certified" by the school that the amount borrowed does not exceed the cost of attendance minus any financial aid. The funds are dispersed directly to the school and usually have lower interest rates.

With direct-to-consumer loans, the school does not certify the cost of attendance, so the student merely provides proof of enrollment, and the funds are dispersed directly to the student. This often results in over-borrowing. Private bank loans usually have variable rates tied to an index like the LIBOR and have up front origination fees, and since most young students have no credit history, the banks push for parents to co-sign. Terms can vary from lender to lender so it pays to shop around. Go to **studentaid.ed.gov**, **studentloans.gov** and **salliemae.com** to learn more.

Even though private student loans are less flexible and more costly than government loans, they enjoy many of the same protections when it comes to default, and are nearly impossible to discharge in bankruptcy court. This means the bankers are much less motivated to work with you if you're struggling to keep up with payments. So never approach student loans with a mindset of "How much can I borrow?" but always with the idea of borrowing only what you need.

Less is better in the long run because student debt can last a long time. The number of consumers 65 years old and up, whose social security benefits were reduced to collect on student loan debt, increased 500% from 2002 to 2013. That's insane!

One quick thing about record keeping. Maintain good records and save your student loan paperwork forever. You don't want to get a call from some bottom-feeding debt collectors five or ten years after graduation saying you owe on an old student loan and have no way to prove them wrong. It happens.

Some closing food for thought (to go with that root beer) just to tick you off. Student loans and ever rising education costs present a chicken-and-egg scenario. Is there more student aid because tuition has increased, or has tuition increased because there is more student aid available? The New York Fed crunched the numbers and determined that federal aid creates a large "pass-through" effect. That means that for every additional $100 dollars the government provides in student loans, colleges and universities increase tuition by $55 to $65. Shame on them.

529 Plans

If you're an older Millennial who's out of school and already have little ones of your own, or thinking of having kids soon, now's the time to start thinking about their education. Just like retirement accounts, there are educational investment accounts that will allow you to take advantage of the miracle of compounding. The vehicle for this is the 529 Plan, named after section 529 of the IRS code. A 529 plan is a tax-advantaged account you can open in your child's name. There are two types: college savings plans and prepaid tuition plans. All fifty states offer at least one of them.

> **Cheers** – The first Millennials were born the year "Cheers," a TV sitcom about a neighborhood bar, premiered. One of the best episodes is when know-it-all Cliff Clavin explained his "Buffalo Theory" to fellow bar-fly Norm Peterson. Here's how it goes:
>
> "Well ya see, Norm, it's like this… A herd of buffalo can only move as fast as the slowest buffalo. And when the herd is hunted, it is the slowest and weakest ones at the back that are killed first. This natural selection is good for the herd as a whole, because the general speed and health of the whole group keeps improving by the regular killing of the weakest members. In much the same way, the human brain can only operate as fast as the slowest brain cells. Excessive intake of alcohol, as we know, kills brain cells. But naturally it attacks the slowest and weakest brain cells first. In this way, regular consumption of beer eliminates the weaker brain cells, making the brain a faster and more efficient machine. That's why you always feel smarter after a few beers."

The college saving plan is similar to an IRA where you put money in, and it grows tax sheltered 'til you need it, and if used for education, withdrawals are tax free. They offer stock and bond investment options and some have age-based portfolios, similar to the target funds we covered in the last chapter, that automatically become more conservative as college age nears.

Some state plans are better than others, because they offer more investment options or have lower fees. Fees are important. A high fee plan might charge you more than $1,800 over eighteen years while charges could be less than $200 at a low fee state. Various magazines and organizations rank these plans, so check them out before you invest. You are not required to use the plan of the state in which you reside, but thirty-three states give limited tax breaks if you do.

But what if, after eighteen years you've save a chunk of change in a 529 and your brilliant teen gets a full ride to Podunk U. No problem. You can use the money for educational expenses for a sibling, cousin, niece, nephew, aunt, uncle, yourself or just about any relative. And if there are none of those whom you want to support, you can have your contributions back tax free. The earnings however would be subject to income tax plus a 10% penalty.

States that offer prepaid tuition plans allow you to lock in tuition prices at certain colleges and universities. Some states even allow you to lock in room and board fees. The down side is that your choice of schools is limited.

Wheels

The third largest purchase for most Millennials will be an automobile. As mentioned earlier, self-discipline is the most difficult thing when it comes to sorting out wants from needs, be it in savings, investing or spending, and nowhere is this more evident than when buying a car.

If you need transportation and head for the dealership unprepared, you will be entering dangerous territory. "The feel of the wheel seals the deal" is an old saying in the auto sales business, and every salesperson's job is to get you to buy as much car as you can afford, or maybe even more. The average car loan is now $29,000 but since there seems to be a psychological hurdle when payments exceed $500 a month, dealers and banks have lengthened the terms of car loans to get more customers behind the wheel of ever more expensive new vehicles. Experian reports the average new-car loan is now 67 months, and J.D. Power says that nearly one-third of new car loans are financed for 72 months or longer, and the fastest growing segment is for auto loans of 73 to 96 months — that's eight years!

Depending on your down payment, you may be upside down (the car is worth less than the loan balance) soon after you drive off the lot, so the lender will require gap insurance to cover the difference in case you total the car. That's no way to fulfill your transportation needs. As a rule of thumb car payments should not exceed 8% of your gross monthly salary or 20% of your monthly take-home pay, and I personally believe if you can't pay off the vehicle in 42 months you need something cheaper because you can't afford it.

When you finally pay off your car loan, don't run out and get a new set of wheels. Instead, with your new-found financial discipline, continue making car payments, except this time you're paying yourself and funding an account for the next one. If you were paying $500 a month, after three years of self-funding your car account, you would have $18,000 toward the next one.

Myanmar, Liberia, and Us – The decimal based metric system started in France in 1799, and has been refined numerous times over the years. The US was founded using the British system of weights and measures but began using the metric system in the early 19th century and officially recognized its use, but did not require it, with the Metric Act of 1866. In 1875, we were one of the original signers of the Metre Convention which created the International Bureau of Weights and Measures in France, and established a standard meter and kilogram for all signatures. Finally in 1893, Thomas Mendenhall, the superintendent of the U S Coast and Geodetic Survey issued the Mendenhall Order which established the kilogram and meter as our standard. But old colonial habits die hard, and we still hang on to our British system, which oddly enough, is now officially defined by the metric system – 1 yard equals 0.9144 meters, 1 mile equals 1.609344 kilometers, 1 acre equals 4046.873 square meters, 1 gallon equals 3.785411784 liters, and on and on. In 1968 the Congress initiated the U S Metric Study which concluded that we should join the rest of the world in using the metric system, and then passed The Metric Conversion Act of 1975 to implement the process. Highway signs were being changed to reflect km/h but unfortunately, budget cuts in the Reagan administration resulted in the project being scraped in 1982, leaving us with a hodgepodge of weights and measures, and joining Liberia and Myanmar as the only non-metric using nations on the planet.

This hodgepodge system where we buy a liter of soda, but a 12 oz. beer and a gallon of gas can have its downside. In December 1998 NASA launched the Mars Climate Orbiter to study the atmosphere of the Red Planet. NASA specified metric units when it let the contract but subcontractor Lockheed Martin apparently didn't get the memo and failed to use metrics in their calculations. NASA intended the spacecraft to orbit at 150 kilometers above the surface but instead it descended to 57 kilometers and burned up in the Martian atmosphere. $327 million went up in smoke. Oops.

The search for lower monthly payments has also driven more people to leasing, and now 27% of customers are leasing instead of purchasing. But is leasing a good deal? Automotive website Edmunds compared the total six year costs for three different ways of getting a mid-sized sedan. They analyzed two back-to-back three year leases with monthly payments of $294; a new vehicle purchase with a 1.64% five-year loan and monthly payments of $400; and a three-year-old used car with a 6% loan and payments of $301. After six years, the total out-of-pocket costs were:

Leasing	$23,476
Buying New	$28,104
Buying Used	$20,364

Of course, at the end of the six years, the person who bought the new car had an auto worth $9,687, and the person who bought the used car had a nine-year-old vehicle worth $4,794 while the lessee has to get a new lease or start walking. So, once you deduct the current value from the out-of-pocket costs, the final cost comes to:

Leasing	$23,476
Buying New	$18,417
Buying Used	$15,570

Unless you're using the vehicle in a business and can use the tax deduction, leasing is penny wise and pound foolish. (See **edmunds.com** for more details.) Just because it allows you to drive a more expensive vehicle is no reason to jump into a lease. The bottom line when it comes to getting a car, like so many other things, is to be disciplined and not bust your budget. Figure out what you can afford and line up your financing before you set foot in a dealership. Then, be strong and don't let "the feel of the wheel..." lull you into getting something that doesn't fit your budget.

The Budget

As we covered in Part I, a written budget allows you to see where your money is going and forces you to prioritize your spending with a goal of living within, or better yet, below your means. It can help spendthrifts sort out wants from needs. When you do your first budget, write in what you actually spent in each category the previous month and come up with budgeting goals for the future, then every month see how you're doing. I'm somewhat reluctant to give exact percentages for each category because each of us is different and have differing priorities. If you research it you'll find numbers all over the map, so use these numbers as a starting point. The important thing is the bottom line, and doing whatever is needed to keep expenses less than income.

Included in this budget, in addition to savings, is what I call a sanity fund. You might call it a vacation fund, or big TV fund, or the remodel-the-bathroom fund, but whatever you call it, you need to put aside some money to enjoy life a little. It also will make it easier for the nearly one fourth of people who are Frugalers to pry open their wallets and spend a few bucks to make a memory.

In these guidelines I'm assuming a single Millennial, or if married, no kids and both spouses working. So, with that said, let's put some meat on the bones of the budget we talked about in Part I. These are percentages of after-tax income.

Savings (Pay yourself first)	10% to 15%
Housing:	
Mortgage/Rent	25% to 30%
Utilities, maintenance	10% to 15%
Transportation:	
Car loan, insurance, gas, maintenance, parking, etc.	15% to 20%
Living:	
Food,	10% to 15%
Clothing, entertainment, health costs, etc.	10% to 15%
Student loans	10%
Sanity fund	5%

Paper or Plastic

Debit cards and credit cards look alike and both provide a convenient way to shop, but there are important differences. Debit cards are digitized versions of your checkbook and prevent you from spending money you don't have. Credit cards on the other hand, have a spending limit based on your credit score, give you better liability protection and may offer perks such as an extended warranty or rewards points. One size doesn't fit all when it comes to plastic, so even though credit cards are better for most of us, debit cards or cash are the better choice for the spendthrifts among us.

When shopping for a credit card, depending on what kind of person you are (know thyself), there are two general types to consider. If you carry a balance every month, which I do not recommend, look for a card with the lowest interest rate. If you pay your balance in full every month, the interest rate isn't important, so shop for a card offering the best rewards. Of course if you do carry a balance for a protracted time, think about a debit card because interest charges can eat you alive.

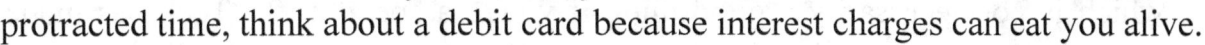

The U.S. lags most of the world when it comes to credit card fraud prevention. To reduce fraud, Eurocard, MasterCard and Visa created the EMV technical standard in the 1990s to replace the easily copied magnetic strips on credit cards with a chip-and-pin system. By 2006 it was in use in most of the world but was not adopted by U.S. banks until 2015, when they introduced the EVM standard but offered chip-and-sign cards that retained the magnetic strip. Go figure! While an improvement, no firm date has been set for using the chip-and-pin-only standard. Here are some of the major differences between credit and debit cards:

	Credit Cards	**Debit Cards**
Spending Limit	Based on credit worthiness.	However much is in your bank account.
Monthly Bill	Yes.	No.
Fees	May have annual fees, late payment fees, overdraw fees.	Can have high overdraft fees.
Interest Charged	Interest charged if balance not paid in full every month.	No interest charged.
Credit History	Responsible usage improves one's credit score.	No effect on credit score.
Fraud Liability	Limited to $50 and usually waived by issuer. Can dispute fraudulent charges.	$50 max when lost/stolen if reported within 48 hours. After 48 hours, the liability is $500. After 60 days, unlimited.
Security	Getting better. Chip and sign is an improvement but chip and pin is even more secure.	Secure as long as no one steals your card number and pin.

Barry Pencek

Never Pay Retail

About a hundred years ago, when famed investor Barnard Baruch was asked the secret to his success he said: "Buy your straw hats in the winter time." When I was a kid my dad used to say, "Never pay retail," which meant you waited for something to go on sale, or out of season, before you bought it. This could take weeks or sometimes months, and patience was required. Today, with the ubiquitous web, you can find the best price in an instant on your smart phone. (One-third of online purchases are now made on mobile devices, which is not necessarily a good thing if you're a spendthrift.) Tech has made shopping entirely too easy, and it feels sooooo good to get a deal — it literally increases endorphins in your brain. Remember that you can go broke saving money. Just because you can get something in a killer sale is not a reason, in and of itself, to buy it if you don't really need it or can't afford it. More than ever, the key to shopping is discipline.

While we're on spending, let me throw a little more Kahneman and Tversky at you. During decision making there is a tendency to rely too heavily on the first piece of information we receive. It's called anchoring and this information may or may not be relevant to the event at hand or the value of an item, but once the anchor is set we develop a cognitive bias and tend to make adjustments relative to the anchor.

> **Big Spenders** – Most of us have spending limits on our credit cards, but not everyone. Billionaire Chinese businessman Liu Yiqian paid $170 million for a Modigliani painting at a Christie's auction and put it on his American Express Black Card saying he and and his family would use the points to travel free for the rest of their lives. (Modigliani lived and died a pauper and would often trade his paintings for food. If he only knew.) It could easily be argued that the painting was a good investment for Yiqian, but other big spenders have made some curious spending decisions:
>
> Nicolas Cage outbid Leonardo DiCaprio and put $276,000 on his card for a dinosaur skull. Huh! Soon after, the IRS came calling for $6 million in unpaid taxes that Cage owed.
>
> Celine Dion put $2 million on her card for a humidifier for her hotel room in Las Vegas to protect her vocal cords from the dry desert air while she slept. Must have been one heck of a machine. They go for $25 to $250 at most big box stores.
>
> Bono left London for Italy without his hat so he bought a $1,700 plane ticket for his lid. I guess he thought

For example, suppose you're at the county sauerkraut festival and come across a tent where they sell life-sized, hand-carved aardvarks with a price tag of $375 (the anchor). You've always wanted a carved aardvark but realize you can't afford to spend that kind of loot. As you start to walk away the old woodcarver tells you that it's your lucky day, because the aardvarks are now on sale for $275. Even though it's going to stretch your finances, you slowly reach for your wallet and pull out the plastic, because everyone loves a deal. Now you're feeling really pumped because this is going to increase your coolness by a factor of a hundred. However, for all you know, he may have been selling the same damn things the day before for a hundred bucks.

In their research, Kahnemann and Tversky asked a group of subjects to multiply 1x2x3x4x5x6x7x8 within five seconds, an impossible task, so the subjects had to guess. Another group was asked to multiply 8x7x6x5x4x3x2x1, again within five seconds. The average estimate for those whose problem began with 1 guessed 512, while those whose problem began with 8 guessed 2250. The first digit was the anchor. (In case you were wondering, the answer for both problems is 40,320.) Besides avoiding the pain of a loss, anchoring is another reason we tend to stick with losing investments too long. We anchor their value at the value they once had — the price we paid when we bought. Anchoring is very hard to avoid, but just being aware of it is a step in the right direction.

---

overnighting it would have been too pedestrian.

Elton John was cautioned by his accountants about racking up credit card charges averaging $400,000 a month. When asked about spending $450,000 for flowers in a twenty month period, the singer replied: "Well, I like flowers." He later had to borrow $40 million against future earnings to pay down debt.

Rapper Drake threw a party for his friend Lil Wayne. The Grey Goose and Dom Perignon flowed like water and the tab at the end of the night was $189,375.

British currency trader Alex Hope threw a party for his friends and ran up a bar tab of $321,000 not including his $30,000 tip.

Beyonce paid $100,000 for a pair of gold Balenciaga leggings to wear on tour.

Russian businessman Roman Abramovich took some friends to lunch at Nello's in New York City. The tab was $47,221 which included a gratuity of $7,328. Two bottles of Cristal Rose and three bottles of La Tache at $5,000 a pop will do that. Abramovich added an extra five grand to the tip which made the total lunch bill $52,221.

Barry Pencek

Never Borrow For Lifestyle

When Queen Victoria married Prince Albert in 1840, she wore a white dress and started a trend among the elites of Europe and America. It was a sign of conspicuous consumption for the masses to witness and dream of emulating. Today weddings are a $100 billion industry in the United States alone, involving 800,000 people including planners, caterers, photographers, florists, jewelers, and even wedding insurance providers. It all started when Marshall Field opened the Bridal Room at their flagship store in Chicago in 1924, which brought the white gown and affordable luxury to the general public. Prior to that a majority of brides wore their best church clothes with black being the most popular color.

Of the two and a half million weddings each year the average cost is about $27,000 but that number is heavily skewed by a small percentage of really high priced events. Of course there are huge regional differences as well, such as $77,000 in NYC vs. $15,000 in Utah, which, ironically averages the largest number of wedding guests at 209. The median cost (half above, half below) is $18,000 but many couples spend less than $10,000.

The tradition of the bride's family paying for the wedding is based on the ancient tradition of a dowry. A dowry originally was a transfer of property to the bride from her family for establishing a household or providing security, but in many cultures evolved to payments directly to the groom or his family. Although dowries are mostly a thing of the past, many

> **The Ring Toss** – Anchoring can have many faces. Back in the seventies I flew an attack helicopter to the North Alabama State Fair in support of the local recruiters. I went wandering down the midway with $40 in my pocket and stopped at a ring-toss booth. The object of the game was to toss rubber rings onto clothespins attached to rows of boards. Each pin had a point value written on the back. I think it was three tosses for five bucks, and if you got 100 points you'd win a prize. I hooked pins on two of my first three throws and when the carny guy pulled the pins he said I got twenty points on each one (the anchor). It was easy peasy so I plopped down another five bucks for three more throws. This time I hooked pins on all three tries but when he showed me the pins they were only worth five points or less. I played on and got a lot of ones, twos and an occasional five, and by the time my money ran out I had ninety points.
>
> I was so pissed I couldn't see straight. I wasn't upset at the carny. I was upset with myself because I had fallen for such an old trick. You see, the game was rigged. All of the pins were worth one to five points. He never showed me the first ones and just told me they were twenties to set the anchor. That bothered me for the next twenty years. As a matter of fact, as I write this forty-some years later, it still kind of ticks me off.

American families look at paying for the wedding as something they want to do for their daughters. In 2014, the bride's parents paid for 43% of wedding costs, the bride and groom contributed 43% and the groom's family covered 12% (2% was kicked in by friends), but this is slowly changing.

As the average age of brides (28 years) and grooms (31 years) increases, many are already established in the workforce and are paying more themselves because they want to make the event more about them and their friends, and less about their parent's friends. The biggest problem is when the couple wants a wedding they can't afford, or runaway costs and add-ons run up the cost. The bottom line is to set a budget and let it drive the event rather than having the wedding tail wag the budget dog. You don't want your first official act as a newly-wed couple to be putting yourselves in debt. It's just not a good way to start a marriage. If you need to borrow for a wedding, you can't afford that wedding.

The same logic goes for travel, be it the royal honeymoon your spouse deserves or a family vacation. Same for that 80-inch ultra hi-def smart television you've had a hankering for. If you need to borrow for these things, don't do it! Delayed gratification is a wonderful thing, so start a savings fund and once you've saved enough, treat yourself and enjoy it debt free.

> **Diamonds Are Forever – Or Not** – Getting married has become expensive. Before World War II, when weddings were much more subdued affairs, only 10% of engagement rings had diamonds in them, while today more than 80% do. A pair of Emory University researchers studied weddings today and found that the more expensive the ring and wedding, the shorter the marriage. They found that when a guy spent between $2,000 and $4,000 on an engagement ring he was 1.3 times as likely to end up in divorce than those who spent $500 to $2,000. And those women whose weddings cost more than $20,000 had a higher divorce rate than those who spent less than $1,000.
>
> Less than a thousand bucks for a wedding! I wondered if that could really happen, and after pondering it for a while, I think it can. Absent just going down to the courthouse, here's how I picture the $1,000 nuptials. First you'll need to have your soberest friend go online and get ordained. Next pick up twenty-two pounds of bean burritos, a few cases of Moon Pies and a keg of Natty Light. Then you and a herd of friends assemble in the front yard, build a bonfire, pick some dandelions, take a lot of selfies, plug in the iPod, and you're ready to go. That covers the ceremony, catering, flowers, entertainment, photos and even lawn maintenance. You may want to rethink the beer and beans around an open flame, but other than that I think you're good.

Barry Pencek
The Talk

Just about everyone has experienced that sometimes uncomfortable moment when the parent awkwardly tries to explain the "birds and the bees" to the adolescent. When it's over, the

parent breathes a sigh of relief and gets to put a check in "the talk" box, and the teen is left wondering why mom or dad was stumbling over what was taught in biology class last year. That talk is all part of growing up, but there's another talk that needs to take place that is too often skipped.

Once you find that perfect mate and fall head over heels in love, don't assume you can live on love for the rest of your lives. The happily-ever-after part requires more than just love. It requires compatibility. Opposites might attract in a lot of areas but when it comes to handling money, it requires "the talk" to make sure you're both singing from the same songbook. Before you even think about tying the knot, y'all both have to fess up about money and debt. What do each of you bring to the financial table. If one of you is a spendthrift, loaded in debt, and the other is a frugalar, you have to sort that out before you go any farther. Finances are one of the leading causes of divorce. It's usually not the lack of money, but disagreement over how to handle money and spending.

DC5

The rock and roll "British Invasion" of the 1960s was led by the Beatles and opened the gates to a deluge of British music and pop culture. The Beatles were soon followed by a plethora of others including The Rolling Stones, The Animals, Herman's Hermits and The Dave Clark Five (also known as DC5), among others. DC5 was the second of the Brit groups to make it on the Ed Sullivan Show, a big-time variety show back in the day of black and white television, which brought them instant fame in the U.S. So what does the Dave Clark Five have to do with spending? Absolutely nothing. I just needed a segue into a couple of guys named Dave and Clark and a few things they have in common.

Dave Ramsey is a nationally syndicated radio and television personality and author focusing on financial advice and helping people get out of debt. National Radio Hall of Fame inductee Clark Howard is also a nationally syndicated radio and television personality, author and consumer advocate who helps people "save more, spend less, and avoid getting ripped off."

Though Howard offers a lot of consumer advice along with financial advice, he and Ramsey seem to agree on several things:

1. Have an "Emergency Fund" of three to six months living expenses.
2. Pay down debt.
3. Invest for retirement.
4. Learn to differentiate wants from needs.
5. Never go into debt for lifestyle.

There is one area however where Clark Howard and Dave Ramsey differ substantially, and that is the use of credit. Dave Ramsey encourages people to pay off all debt and live a cash-only lifestyle while Clark Howard encourages people to wisely use credit to their advantage. So who's right? Well, as you might have guessed, it depends on the person. As we've seen, credit can be your best friend or worst enemy. It's another reason to "know

> **Prime Ain't Just Beef** – In culinary circles "US Prime" refers to the highest quality beef and is followed by "choice," "select," "standard," and "commercial" grades. Those grades are actually followed by "utility," "cutter," and "canner" grades which are usually not sold as cut meat in food-service operations but are typically ground up and used in canned products. (Potted meat anyone?)
>
> In financial circles "US Prime" refers to the interest rate banks charge their most credit-worthy customers. Individual banks determine their prime rate by adding about 3% to the Federal Funds Rate, a rate banks charge each other for overnight loans that is set by the Federal Reserve. (The banks add anywhere from 2% to 4% but it averages 3%)
>
> The prime rate is used as a basis for credit card rates, small business loans, home equity lines of credit and other lending. The Wall Street Journal publishes an unofficial national benchmark called the WSJ Prime by surveying the 30 largest banks and averaging their responses. With globalization, fewer loans are now tied to the US Prime rate and more are tied to the LIBOR, or London Interbank Offered Rate. LIBOR is the global standard used when large international banks lend money to each other and is published daily by the British Bankers' Association (BBA). The BBA surveys 18 major global banks daily and publishes the average in 10 different currencies for 15 different maturities, ranging from one day to one year, the most common being the one month, three month, six month, and one year rates. LIBOR is an ever more widely used benchmark, especially for mortgages.

thyself." If you tend to be a spendthrift and money burns a hole in your pocket then you need plastic surgery, and cash and debit cards are the way to go. If on the other hand, you're more disciplined, then the wise use of credit will help you borrow money closer to the "prime" rate and get better deals on everything from mortgages, to car loans, to insurance policies. Part of knowing yourself is knowing how you're viewed by the rest of the world and when it comes to things financial, that's your credit report and credit score.

Credit Reports

Your credit report is your credit history as reported to credit agencies by those who have extended credit to you. Your occupation, salary, and employment history are not part of it, so in reality your credit report doesn't show your ability to pay debt, but rather your willingness to pay, based on your history of paying bills on time.

Businesses use credit reports to assess the risk of extending credit to an individual but your report also plays a big role in determining your interest rate on a loan, the amount of rent you'll pay, your insurance premium and even if you get that job you applied for.

There are three nationwide credit reporting agencies (CRAs) that collect data on us: Equifax, Experian and TransUnion, and under federal law, you're entitled to one free credit report every year from each of them. Go to **annualcreditreport.com** to get your credit report. Beware of other websites advertising free credit reports, they usually require you to sign up for a credit monitoring service which you have to pay for. You can check with all three agencies once a year or you may want to monitor your report throughout the year by checking with a different bureau every four months. If there should be a problem, there will be a number to call on your report or you can reach the agencies at the following addresses:

Equifax	Experian	TransUnion
P O Box 740241	P O Box 9554	P O Box 6790
Atlanta, GA 30374	Allen, TX 75013	Fullerton, CA 92834
www.equifax.com	www.experian.com	www.transunion.com
800.685.1111	888.397.3742	800.888.4213
800.525.6285		800.680.7289

If you've ever pulled your credit report and gotten the feeling that big brother was watching, you ain't seen nothin yet. In addition to the three big national bureaus, there are dozens of specialty consumer reporting agencies that provide information about you that deal with salary, driving record, paying your rent on time, police records, medical conditions, gambling, legal filings, and even how often you return products to merchants.

All of these agencies will also provide a copy of your report every year. Some charge a fee (maximum of $12) and some are free. The chart below shows these agencies and which ones are free. You can learn more about what these specialty agencies look at, plus get contact information and find out how to request a report at the Consumer

EMPLOYMENT SCREENING		PERSONAL PROPERTY INSURANCE	
Accurate Background		C.L.U.E. Inc.	Free
American DataBank		Drivers History	
backgroundchecks.com		Insurance Information Exchange	
EmployeeScreen IQ	Free	Insurance Services Office, Inc	
First Advantage Corporation	Free		
General Information Services	Free	MEDICAL	
HireRight	Free	MIB, Inc	Free
Info Cubic		Milliman Intelliscript	
IntelliCorp			
OPENonline		LOW INCOME and SUBPRIME	
Pre-employ.com	Free	Clarity Services	Free
SterlingBackcheck	Free	Data X	Free
Trak 1		Factor Plus	Free
The Work Number	Free	MicroBilt/PRBC	Free
		CoreLogic Teletrack	Free
TENANT SCREENING		SUPPLEMENTARY REPORTS	
Contemporary Information Corp			
CoreLogic SafeRent	Free	CoreLogic Credco	Free
Experian RentBureau	Free	Innovis	Free
First Advantage Corporation	Free	LexisNexis Risk Solutions	Free
LeasingDesk		SageStream	Free
Screening Reports, Inc.		UTILITIES	
Tenant Data Services		Nat'l Consumer Telecom & Utility	Free
TransUnion Rental Screening			
		RETAIL	
CHECK AND BANK SCREENING		The Retail Equation	
Certegy Check Services	Free		
ChexSystems	Free	GAMING	
Early Warning Services	Free	Certegy Gaming Services	Free
TeleCheck Services	Free		

Financial Protection Bureau. Go to **consumerfinance.gov** and search for *specialty consumer reporting agencies*. (It's a PDF document.)

All credit agencies, including specialty agencies, are required to give you a copy of your report if you receive an *adverse action notice*, such as being turned down for a loan. In the *adverse action notice* the lender has to tell you the name of the agency from which it got your report and how to contact them.

In all credit scoring models, paying your bills on time and the amount of outstanding debt are the biggest players, so it's important for you to be conscientious about these or it can end up as a negative item in your report. You can correct errors on your report but you cannot remove negative information if it's true. Most negative information stays on your report for seven years, bankruptcy for ten years, and judgments can stay until the statute of limitations runs out. But like all rules there are exceptions. According to the Fair Credit Reporting Act (section 605), although the CRAs normally cannot report negative information after seven years, they can keep it in their records. And it can be reported when there's an inquiry in regards to a loan or insurance policy greater than $150,000 or a job paying more than $75,000. However after seven years the information is pretty stale and shouldn't carry much weight, except perhaps for very sensitive jobs or those requiring a security clearance.

Credit Scores

Engineer William Fair and mathematician Earl Issac founded Fair, Issac and Company in 1956 and began selling their first risk assessment system to lenders two years later. In 1989 they introduced the general purpose FICO credit score. Today it's a billion dollar corporation operating in 20 countries and the FICO score is considered the gold standard of risk assessment by lenders.

FICO doesn't give away the secret recipe for their scoring model but generally scores are broken down as follows: 35% is based on payment history, 30% amount owed, 15% length of credit history, 10% credit mix, and 10% new credit. The generic FICO scores range from 300 to 850 but you may receive different scores from each of the three national reporting agencies as well as the specialty agencies because they each have their own scoring models too.

To further confuse the issue, a few industries use different ranges — for example the auto and bankcard industries use a range of 250 to 900 on their FICO scores. If a lender provides you with a copy of your credit score it can sometimes get confusing because over the years there have been various models and sometimes the CRAs have given them their own names. So if you receive a Beacon, NextGen, Pinnacle, Empirica, or Precision score, it's FICO.

Some things that are not part of your credit score are: Salary, occupation, age, race, religion, marital status, sex, or nation of origin. So a rhino trainer making $40,000 a year could have a great score while the rock star pulling in $4 million might have lousy numbers.

In 2006, the big three CRAs got tired of paying Fair Issac and decided to create their own credit score called VantageScore with a range of 501 to 990. Fortunately for us, in 2013 they released VantageScore 3.0 and changed the range to 300 to 850 so it matched FICO which eliminated a lot of confusion. VantageScore weightings are slightly different from FICO with payment history making up 40% of the score, debt-to-credit ratio 21%, total debt 20%, length of history 11%, recent credit 5% and available credit 3%.

So what is a good credit score? Each CRA and each lender has their own definition but as a general guideline this will get you in the ballpark. Less than 600 is really bad; 600-649 poor; 650-699 fair; 700-749 good; and 750 and higher is excellent. In case you were wondering, according to Experian the average VantageScore for consumers is 669.

While your credit report is free, you must pay for your credit score if you want it from FICO or one of the big three CRAs, however numerous third party websites allow you to get your VantageScore at no cost. The most popular are **creditkarma.com** and **quizzle.com** but others include **credit.com**, **creditsesame.com**, **lendingtree.com** and **mint.com**. These sites allow you to check your score weekly or monthly but usually include advertising for you to enjoy while you're on their site.

Insurance

If someone depends on you financially, you need to have life insurance. The amount of life insurance is determined by how big your financial obligations are. The industry rule of thumb is that you should have a death benefit of seven to ten times your annual income, so if you make $50,000 a year you will need $350,000 to $500,000 in life insurance, but in my opinion that one-size-fits-all approach is lacking. If you're single and renting an apartment, all you need is enough to bury you, pay your debts and maybe something for your favorite charity. But if you're married, you'll need to replace some or all of your income. If you and your spouse have a mortgage, you'll need additional coverage. Get a

TR Saves Football – Growing up in New York City Teddy was a sickly little kid but had a sharp mind, and in 1876 attended Harvard. He became a big fan of the relatively new game of football but was too nearsighted to play, so he took up boxing instead. Later he moved to the badlands of North Dakota and learned to ride, rope and hunt, and the sickly little city boy became a bad-ass cowboy.

When college football started it was nothing like the game played today. It was a cross between soccer and rugby, and the home school set the rules. So some schools met in 1873 to standardize things. There were 20 players on each side, and the game was played on a field 400 x 250 feet. Play began with a scrum using a round ball which could be kicked or batted with the hands or head but not picked up.

Harvard did not adopt these rules and played a rugby-style game which allowed for the ball to be carried. Other schools followed Harvard's lead and in 1880, Yale player Walter Camp got the rules changed to reduce each team to 11 players and replaced the scrum with the "snap." In 1882 "downs" were added, the field was shrunk to 110 yards, and lines were drawn every five yards that resembled a gridiron. A scoring system allowed four points for a touchdown, two for a safety and "goal following a touchdown," and five points for "goal from field."

Football was a very brutal sport. In 1905 nineteen college players died and more than 150 were badly injured. Several schools dropped the sport or switched to rugby, which they considered safer. Newspapers across the country, along with Harvard president Charles Elliot, called for the sport to be banned. In stepped Teddy Roosevelt, the bad-ass cowboy from New York who was now President. He said rules were needed to "minimize the danger" as long as the game didn't become "too lady-like," so sixty-two schools met that December and formed what would become the NCAA. The forward pass was made legal, many of today's rules were adopted, and the game survived. FYI: Although many players wore various types of leather helmets, they weren't mandatory till 1939.

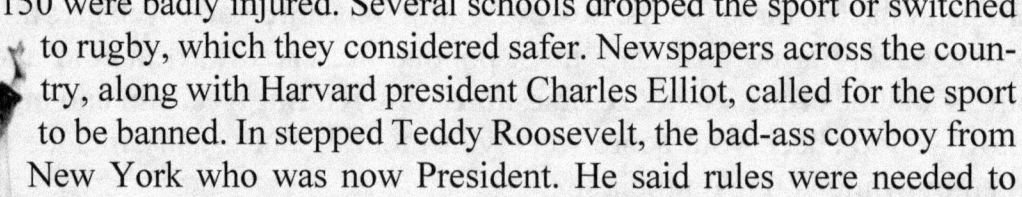
Testing football helmets, 1912.

pay raise, add some more. Have kids and you really need more insurance since it costs around a quarter million to raise a child, and that's not counting college. Most young parents today are under-insured, but the good news is that if you're young and in good health, life insurance is very inexpensive.

There are two basic types of life insurance, term and permanent. Term life is simple. Just like auto or homeowners insurance, you pay the premium for the year, and if you have a claim they cover it, but if you don't have a claim the money is gone. If you don't have a claim, don't think the money was wasted because not having a life insurance claim means that you're still breathing and looking at the grass from the topside, which is good. Term policies are for a fixed period of time, most commonly 10, 20 or 30 years and may come with conversion and renewable options. Renewability allows you to extend the policy without having to pass a physical, though sometimes for only one more term. Convertibility means the policy can be exchanged for a permanent life policy without a medical exam, however premiums for these options increase accordingly.

Permanent insurance generally comes in three flavors — whole life, universal life and variable life — and provides permanent protection, which is good should you ever develop a medical condition that might preclude you from getting term insurance. Permanent insurance is much more expensive and combines a death benefit with a savings component, and never expires as long as the premiums are paid.

Whole life, the most expensive type, provides a fixed death benefit and minimum guaranteed interest rate for the savings portion. With universal life the death benefit and investment portions are separated and some flexibility is provided which allows the death benefit, and thereby the premium, to be changed if a policyholder's situation changes. Less common is variable life which entails some investment risk because the investment portion can be invested in stocks, bonds, and mutual funds.

Many companies provide life insurance for their employees, but if you only have employer provided coverage and leave your job, you'll find yourself without coverage and that's not good. So don't count employer coverage when figuring your insurance needs. Here are a few guidelines for when you go shopping for insurance:

1. Buy a 30-year term policy as your base coverage and make sure it has a convertible feature in case you ever develop a medical condition and need permanent life insurance.

2. Never buy any type of cash value policy as an investment. You'll do better putting the excess premium in an index fund.

3. A non-working spouse needs life insurance too, especially when there are children, to cover daycare and other expenses.

4. Review your coverage every time you have a lifestyle change. Consider laddering several policies, for example every time you add a child to the family you could get an additional 20 year level term policy for $250,000. It's just to get the kids out of the nest so you won't need a convertible or renewable feature.

5. Check out the financial health of insurance companies at insurance rating company AM Best, because your policy is only as solid as the company behind it. Look for an A++ or A+ rating.

6. Policies have pricing break-points at $100,000, $250,000, $500,000 and $1 million, so a $250,000 policy is just a few bucks more than one for $200,000.

Retirement Spending

Many, if not most, Gen Xers think there will be no money in the Social Security coffers when their turn comes, and as you Millennials get older and learn more about retirement, I'm sure large numbers of you will feel the same way. Social Security has run a surplus for decades but with so many Boomers retiring, the system now runs a deficit, and they will empty the till around 2035. Because they're so busy arguing and pointing fingers, it's unlikely the Gang of 535 (100 in the Senate and 435 in the House) will do anything until things get to a crisis situation, but eventually they'll get around to dealing with the issue, or risk a revolt of the blue-hairs, who vote in large numbers. But even if the pols in DC did nothing and the well ran dry, Social Security taxes would cover about three quarters of benefits, so don't worry too much, I think there will at least be some dregs left for y'all.

Of the 10,000 Boomers retiring every day, half of them have saved less than $50,000 toward retirement and a fourth have saved nothing. I know you'll avoid a similar fate because you have now established your saving and investing strategies, and are on your way to a much more secure future. I also realize you're a long way from retirement, but everyone eventually retires and needs a plan for spending their savings wisely, so you don't outlive your money. As food for thought, or in case you have to help your parents or grandparents with retirement planning, I offer a few options.

The 4% Rule — Conceived in 1994 by William Bengen, an MIT educated aeronautical engineer turned financial planner. He determined that if you withdrew 4% of your portfolio annually, and increased that dollar amount by the rate of inflation each year, your money would last from 33 years to 50 years, depending on economic conditions. His research included various asset allocations but concluded you're best served with at least 50%, but not more than 75%, in stocks and the rest in bonds. Critics claim the plan lacks flexibility.

Buckets of Money – The so-called bucket strategy is the brainchild of famous financial planner Harold Evensky, and has retirement assets divided up into various "buckets" — usually three — and allocated based on the time period when the funds will be used and the retiree's tolerance for risk. The first bucket is for short-term needs and contains cash or cash equivalents necessary for the next three to five years and is structured to minimize risk and not lose value. Next is the intermediate-term bucket which contains fixed-income securities with a time frame of up to 15 years out. The long-term bucket contains equities, which are usually more volatile investments (but as we know risk diminishes with increasing time-spans) and are meant for needs beyond 15 years and to keep the portfolio ahead of inflation. Re-balancing the stocks in bucket three once or twice a year allows dividends and capital gains to replenish bucket two and interest from bucket two spills into bucket one.

Dividends and Interest Only – Not an optimal solution for most investors since dividends are not guaranteed and interest rates can fluctuate and may not meet your spending needs. However if your retirement accounts are over-funded and you're rolling in the dough, it would probably provide all the money you need.

---

222 to Zip – The most lopsided score in the history of college football occurred in October 1916, when Georgia Tech defeated the Cumberland Bulldogs of Lebanon, Tennessee 222 to 0. Of course, there's a story behind this record setting event. Cumberland, which had discontinued football the year before, had previously scheduled Tech and coach John Heisman insisted they show up for the game. Heisman was also the baseball coach and had lost to Cumberland 22 – 0 amidst allegations Cumberland used professionals as ringers, and the coach wanted to avenge that loss on the gridiron.

Heisman sent a letter to Cumberland stating they would have to pay $3,000 to cover lost gate revenue if they failed to show, but if they came he would give them $500 plus expenses. George Allen, the manager of the baseball team, got a dozen or so of his frat brothers together and went to Atlanta. The Bulldogs never had a first down, and neither did Tech; they scored on every possession. Neither team threw a pass, and Tech amassed 978 yards on the ground while Cumberland had minus 28. Tech was leading 126 to 0 at the half when Coach Heisman told his players: "You're doing all right team, we're ahead. But you just can't tell what those Cumberland players have up their sleeves. They may spring a surprise. Be alert men! Hit 'em clean, but hit 'em hard." By the fourth quarter, the Bulldogs were punting on first down to keep from getting injured.

RMD Strategy — Another spend-down strategy is to use the Required Minimum Distribution (RMD) life expectancy tables published by the IRS (Publication 590B) to compute IRA withdrawals. As an example, if you're 65 years old the tables say you have a life expectancy of 21 years, so you divide your portfolio by 21 to determine your withdrawal for the year. (At 100, the IRS says you have 2.9 years left and at 110, you're good for another 1.1 years. Wow!) One Vanguard study found that a RMD strategy coupled with an immediate annuity produced more stable returns than other strategies.

Annuities – An annuity is a tax deferred insurance contract whereby you give an insurance company a sum of money, either a lump sum or payments over time, and receive guaranteed payments, usually for the rest of your life, or even your spouse's life. It may be immediate, in which case you give the insurance company a lump sum payment and start receiving payments immediately, or it can be deferred, where there is an accumulation phase where you pay in over time and then begin receiving payments at some date in the future.

There are fixed and variable annuities. The fixed annuity pays a fixed interest rate or can be linked to an index such as the S&P 500 with a guaranteed minimum rate. With a variable annuity the return will rise and fall with the performance of your chosen portfolio, just like a stock or mutual fund, and performance is not guaranteed.

One common complaint about annuities is that they have high fees, plus deferred annuities will have surrender charges if you want to get out of the contract for the first five to ten years. To get around this you can buy *direct-sold* fixed annuities through fund companies such as Vanguard, Fidelity, Schwab, TIAA and T Rowe Price without commissions or surrender charges.

One last thing. An annuity is not backed by the FDIC and is only as secure as the insurance company from which you purchase it, so check out a company with A.M. Best, Moody's, Fitch, or Standard and Poors to see that they are top rated. (More than 70 insurance companies have gone into receivership since 1983.) An immediate annuity may be appropriate for a portion (no more than 25%) of a retirement portfolio but you should always be mindful of costs and compare offers.

I Want it, and I Want it Now!

The little candy in the pantry experiment with my boys that I told you about in Part I was not an entirely original idea. It was similar to famous experiments by psychologist Walter Mischel of Stanford in the 1960s and 1970s when he was investigating delayed gratification and self control. In those studies small children ages three to six were provided a treat, usually a cookie, pretzel or marshmallow, and told they could eat it immediately or wait 15 minutes and get a second treat. A few kids ate the treat immediately but most anguished over the temptation and held out for a while. In the end about one-third of the subjects were able to wait the entire 15 minutes. He carried out this test on 600 children over several years and other researchers repeated it in other countries and cultures with similar results. (Check out *marshmallow tests* on YouTube for some hilarious video of the kids.)

Read My Lips – In 1988, German music producer Frank Farian created a rap album using a number of vocalists. Farian decided the singers weren't very marketable so he hired a couple of dancer/models named Robert Pilatus and Fabrice Morvan to lip-sync the songs on stage. He called the duo Milli Vanilli. The album was released in 1989 and became an instant success earning a Best New Artist Grammy for the guys. All went well until a technical hiccup caused the soundtrack to skip and repeat at a live MTV concert in Connecticut. Oops! The guys panicked, ran off stage and faded away. The duo later returned their Grammy, but hey, they were good dancers.

Lip syncing isn't all that rare. Mariah Cary, Shakira, Britney Spears, Lindsay Lohan, and Beyonce, have all been accused of it, but at least they actually recorded the tracks and could sing.

Back before the earth cooled, in the middle of the last century, musicals were really big on the silver screen, but some big film stars couldn't carry a tune in a bucket. No problemo! In would step soprano Marni Nixon. She provided the singing voices for Margaret O'Brian in *The Secret Garden* (1949), Marilyn Monroe (high notes only) in *Gentlemen Prefer Blonds* (1953), Deborah Kerr in *The King and I* (1956) and *An Affair to Remember* (1957), Natalie Wood and Rita Moreno in *West Side Story* (1961), Natilie Wood in *Gypsy* (1962), and Audrey Hepburn in *My Fair Lady* (1962). Nixon asked for but never received any credits or royalties for her work. (The soundtrack for *West Side Story* sold more than three million copies.) Finally in 1965 she got her one and only onscreen singing part as Sister Sophia in *The Sound of Music*. Dubbed (pun intended) "the ghostess with the mostest" by Time magazine, she went on to perform on Broadway and as a soloist with philharmonic orchestras and in opera houses around the world. Marni Nixon died in July, 2016.

Mischel followed the subjects for the next 40 years and the results were quite amazing. The longer the subject was able to delay gratification during the test, the better were outcomes later in life, including higher SAT scores and earnings, better social skills, healthier, happier lives, plus less drug addition, obesity and incarceration. Brain scans in 2011 of some of the original participants showed more activity in the prefrontal cortex (so better executive function) of those who withstood temptation the longest when they were five years old.

So Millennials, ask yourself this: Were you in line at one minute past midnight to see *Star Wars: The Force Awakens,* on the day it was released? Were you willing to pay extra for immediate delivery of the latest *Madden NFL* or *Call of Duty: Black Ops*? Do you need the latest iPhone, even though you're only half way through your contract? If this describes you, the good news is that this behavior can be modified and you can improve your self-discipline. Start by promising yourself something small, like saving for your own "marshmallow" and then buying it instead of borrowing for it. Then repeat this behavior over and over and over again with ever larger "treats" until you've trained your brain to accept the wait. Eventually your self-discipline will strengthen and the need for instant gratification will lesson. Now put down that joystick and get started. And pour yourself a root beer while you're at it. Just remember that we humans buy things based on emotion, then justify it with logic, especially the marshmallow eaters among us. That's why the feel of the wheel so often seals the deal. Be strong!

The Big, Warm Fuzzy

If you had the cash to pay off a debt that had a 4% interest rate — be it a mortgage, car loan, or any other obligation — but could earn 5% if you invested the money instead, should you do it? Basic math and logic says to invest the money and enjoy the spread. But there's an intangible that can't be quantified in dollar terms, and that's the big warm fuzzy feeling you get when you no longer owe on your car, or house, or anything, and you're totally debt free. You feel a sense of accomplishment, and elation that's difficult to describe, let alone put a price tag on.

As a Millennial you might not be ready to pay off a mortgage but you can still get a warm fuzzy by paying off your credit cards, or car loan, or just by getting your financial house in order. Once you establish your goals, set up a saving and investing plan to achieve them, and get your spending on firm footing, as you begin to see progress toward achieving financial independence you're going to experience your own big warm fuzzy. The most important thing is to take the first steps and begin the journey. Doing nothing is not an option, so get to it!

The Bottom Line

What have we learned about spending?

-- When a windfall brings sudden wealth, lots of discipline is needed or you'll blow it.

-- You can get out of debt if you're willing to change your ways.

-- You need to be smart about education. Student loans are killing the Millennial generation.

-- If you go to college, pursue a degree in something you're passionate about but something you can make a living with.

-- Do your homework before buying a car and separate wants from needs.

-- Always keep a written budget.

-- "Know thyself" when choosing a debit or credit card.

-- Be aware of anchoring.

-- Never borrow for lifestyle.

-- You need to jealously protect your credit.

-- Term life insurance is usually the best option.

-- Work on delayed gratification, it will save you a bundle of money.

Part IV

Living

Wealth: (noun) An abundance or profusion of anything; plentiful amount.
dictionary.com

"Each man should give what he has decided in his heart to give, not reluctantly or under compulsion, for God loves a cheerful giver."
2 Corinthians 9:7

"Give a man a fish; he'll eat for a day. Teach a man to fish; he'll eat for life."
Chinese proverb

"Great minds discuss ideas; average minds discuss events; small minds discuss people."
Eleanor Roosevelt

"...ask not what your country can do for you, ask what you can do for your country."
John F Kennedy

"... the catastrophe that awaits everyone from a single false move, wrong turn, fatal encounter. Every life has such a moment. What distinguishes us is whether – and how – we ever come back."
Charles Krauthammer, MD
Journalist

"I certainly don't want to leave them trust funds that are albatrosses around their necks."
Sting
British singer

"Train people well enough so they can leave, treat them well enough so they don't want to."
Richard Branson
Entrepreneur

"Climb the mountain so you can see the world, not so the world can see you..."
David McCullough

I cried because I had no shoes, then I met a man who had no feet.
Persian proverb

"He was a wise man who invented beer."
Plato

The Big Picture

Congrats! You're almost done. Graduation is just a chapter away. Now we're going to look at stuff somewhat removed from personal finance, but things that hopefully will lead you to a happier, healthier and more fulfilling life. We'll delve into personal qualities such as happiness, virtue, and service plus other things like leadership, health, and being better prepared for the zombie apocalypse or whatever life throws at you. Think of it as advice from an older generation and take it for what it's worth.

What is Wealth?

Most definitions of wealth refer to money or material possessions, yet many people – who are not what some would regard as wealthy – consider themselves blessed with riches. Others have large paychecks and live luxurious lifestyles but in fact, also are not wealthy. If you were to drive through the McMansionville section of any U.S. city with the luxury cars parked in the driveway, and could somehow see the assets and liabilities of those living there, you'd discover that many are living paycheck to paycheck and well beyond their means.

So say professors Thomas Stanley and William Danko, authors of **The Millionaire Next Door**, who tell us that wealth and income are two different things. They say monetary wealth is not about what you spend, but what you accumulate, and in their research of wealthy individuals, they classify them as Prodigious Accumulators of Wealth (PAWs) or Under Accumulators of Wealth (UAWs).

Stanley and Danko came up with a formula so you could see where you fit. Multiply your age by your pretax income from all sources, and divide by ten to get your expected net worth. If your actual accumulated wealth is double the expected net worth, you're a PAW, and if it's half of it, you're a UAW. Using their formula, a 40 year old earning $50,000 a year who has accumulated $400,000 in assets would be a PAW and considered wealthy, while a 40 year old earning $200,000 a year and having $400,000 in assets would be a UAW. So you might be *wealthy* and not even know it. While their formula deals with monetary wealth, we'll see later that there are many things more important than money. But for now, get out your calculator and see how you're doing.

Sometimes wealth is less about how good an accumulator you are and more about how lucky you are. Billionaire Michael Bloomberg says that most of what successful people in history have achieved, including himself, was due more to luck than any special talent or skill they possessed. They happened to be in the right place at the right time. To a certain extent, history bears him out, but you still need to have your act together and be prepared to seize the moment should opportunity, large or small, knock on your door.

Can Money Buy Happiness?

Think of laughing peasants and billionaires on Prozac. If accumulating money was all there was to happiness, this wouldn't happen, yet it does. That's not to say that the lack of money doesn't make life more painful. Of course there's research on this subject too, (Is there anything someone hasn't researched?) and wouldn't you know it involves our friend, Daniel Kahneman. This time he hooked up with fellow Princeton prof. Angus Deaton and they discovered that day to day happiness increased with income up to about $75,000 a year

---

Super-rich – Here are some of the wealthiest people of all time. (Their wealth is adjusted for inflation and in U.S. dollars.) It's from a list of the 75 richest people in human history found in *Outliers* by Michael Gladwell. Astonishingly, 20% of the names on his list were all from one country and born within nine years of one another. Those were born in the 1830s in America, came of age when railroads were being built, Wall Street was emerging, and the country was transitioning to an industrial economy. These guys were in the right place at the right time and took advantage of it. (The list was compiled before Sam Walton died.)

1.	John D. Rockefeller	$318.3B	U.S.	Standard Oil
2.	Andrew Carnegie	$298.3B	U.S.	Carnegie Steel
3.	Czar Nicholas II	$253.5B	Russia	House Romanov
4.	William H. Vanderbilt	$231.6B	U.S.	Railroads
5.	Osman Ali Khan, Asaf Jah VII	$210.8B	Hyderabad	Monarch
6.	Andrew W. Mellon	$188.8B	U.S.	Gulf Oil
7.	Henry Ford	$188.1B	U.S.	Ford Motors
8.	Marcus Licinius Crassius	$169.8B	Rome	Roman Senate
9.	Basil II	$169.4B	Byzantine Empire	Monarch
10.	Cornelius Vanderbilt	$167.4B	U.S.	Railroads
17.	Sam Walton	$128.9B	U.S.	Wal-Mart
21.	Cleopatra	$ 98.0B	Egypt	Ptolemaic Queen
31.	Carlos Slim	$ 72.4B	Mexico	Telemex
37.	Bill Gates	$ 58.0B	U.S.	Mircosoft
41.	Warren Buffett	$ 52.4B	U.S.	Berkshire Hathaway

and then plateaued. However, satisfaction with life, or one's sense of success, continues to increase with income. Other research shows that spending money on life experiences brings us greater pleasure that lasts longer than the acquisition of material things. Buying that big screen television will make you happy for a while, but the happiness fades long before the picture, so you're better off spending more money doing things with friends and family instead of buying things.

Another way you can have more happiness with money is by giving some of it away. In 2010, Bill Gates and his friend Warren Buffet hatched a scheme over dinner to get America's billionaires to pledge a majority of their wealth to charity. Buffet himself pledged 99% of his wealth, and to this day says: "I couldn't be happier with that decision." You don't have to be a gazillionaire to get in on the act. The pleasure received from helping a stranger in need lasts longer than that gotten from buying a new pair of shoes for yourself.

Too many of us define happiness based on images developed for us by society – the beautiful spouse, big house, fancy clothes, expensive car – but in reality you'll always be chasing a pipe dream and will never be able to live up to unrealistic expectations. Life is too short to get too caught up in accumulating "things" instead of going out and making memories.

Virtue

"It is money, it is money, it is money, it is [expletive] money" Peanut Corporation of America CEO Stewart Parnell wrote in an email in 2007, after knowingly shipping salmonella contaminated peanut butter that killed nine and sickened more than 700 people across the country. Mr. Parnell was so consumed by greed that he faked lab tests to show the product was safe, even after being questioned by inspectors. That dirt ball now has the next 28 years, living in a gated community, to think about his actions.

Doing what's right isn't always easy. In his book ***The Road to Character***, New York Times columnist and political pundit, David Brooks writes about two different virtues that most people have. He calls them resume virtues and eulogy virtues, the former being the education, job history, accomplishments and skills one might bring to a job interview, while the latter are the virtues people will discuss at your funeral and for which you'll be remembered. Were you a good person, an honest person, a kind person, and did you help others? Most of us don't think about the eulogy virtues enough because we're too busy concentrating on the resume virtues, but in the end, it's the eulogy virtues that are really most important in life. Contrast Mr. Parnell's behavior to that of a person like Jimmy Carter. He was a middling president (resume virtues) but a great person (eulogy virtues) who found meaning in using his position to help others.

Victor Frankl was a neurologist and psychiatrist from Vienna who discovered first hand a deeper understanding of what's important in life. During World War II he went from being world renowned in his field to nothing but a number - 119,104. When he was first sent to the Auschwitz concentration camp for processing, his goal was to keep the scientific manuscript of his life's work that he had spent years writing and was hiding in the lining of his coat. Only after he was standing naked in a room with a group of other men did it hit him that not only did he not have his manuscript, but no coat, nor watch, nor wedding ring, nor even hair, since their bodies had been shaved. All he possessed was his naked existence with no material link to his former life. He was later able to get back his glasses and a belt which he traded for a piece of bread, but had come to the realization that his former life was over.

> **The Big M** – In 1940, Dick and Maurice "Mac" McDonald opened McDonald's Bar-B-Que in San Bernardino, California complete with carhops and a menu of burgers, dogs and barbecue, and a goal of making $1 million each. The brothers soon realized that most of their profits were coming from burgers and began to brainstorm how they could provide faster service at a lower cost. In 1948 they closed the restaurant for remodeling, got rid of the carhops, simplified the menu, and implemented their "speedy service system" which they had designed for standardization and maximum efficiency. The makeover included two golden arches on the exterior. Business boomed, and they opened their first franchised location in Phoenix in 1953. By 1954 they had 15 locations and hired a milkshake machine salesman and visionary named Ray Kroc to handle the franchising workload.
>
> In 1961, Kroc purchased the business for $2.7 million, and the brothers each received around $1 million after taxes. An interesting part of the deal was an alleged handshake agreement that the brothers would receive one half of one percent of gross sales annually and got to keep the original restaurant which they renamed The Big M. After closing the deal, Kroc reportedly reneged on the agreement, cheating the brothers out of hundreds of millions of dollars, and then put a McDonald's across from The Big M to drive them out of business.

Though his wife, parents, and brother all perished, Frankl survived the concentration camps and went on to a distinguished career in psychotherapy and to write extensively of our need for meaning in life. He wrote that there is no blanket meaning-of-life that applies to everyone, but that it's up to each of us to discover what gives our life meaning. We need to find our meaning-in-life, and it's different for each of us. All life involves suffering somewhere along the way, and by finding what gives one's life meaning, you can better handle whatever hand life deals you. If you have a "why" to live, you can cope with almost any "how." Frankl died in 1997 at age 92.

I once ran into a forest ranger while hiking in the Bob Marshall Wilderness Area of Montana. During the summers he was working on his PhD in forestry; the rest of the time he spent living in a cabin in the wilderness and would actually spend about fifteen nights a month sleeping out in the woods. Perhaps not the job that most of us dream about, but here was a well-educated person who found his meaning in life and was doing what he loved. We should all be so lucky. It doesn't matter if you want to teach, preach, fly, dance

---

A Grande Dame – Lila Daughtry Denmark was born in 1898, and lived to the ripe old age of 114 years and 60 days, making her the fifth oldest living person in the world at the time of her death in 2012. But she was no ordinary woman and is noted more for her accomplishments in medicine than her age. She was the only female in the graduating class of 1928 at the Medical College of Georgia, and became a pioneering pediatrician and medical researcher, receiving the Fisher Award in 1935 for her work in developing the pertussis (whooping cough) vaccine.

Dr. Denmark worked out of her home in Atlanta and a visit to her office was unique by today's standards. You would walk into a small waiting room and put your name on a sign-in sheet. There were no receptionists, nurses or other staff in the office. She would come out and take the next person on the list. The visit might last ten minutes or 45 minutes, depending on your needs. When needed, she would take a drop of blood from a baby's finger and put it on a slide and look at it under her microscope to do a blood count. (She once told me a microscope salesman came to her office offering to take her to lunch, but she politely told the young man that first, she didn't eat lunch, and second, her microscope worked just as well then as it did in 1928 when she bought it.)

When Rod was a baby, office visits were $4 but by the time she retired they were up to a whopping $10. Dr Denmark saw patients till she was 103, becoming the oldest practicing physician in America, and never hesitated to dispense child-rearing advice or answer questions. She was an advocate of common sense and preventative medicine. You can learn more at **http://drleiladenmark.com/** and get a look at this grande dame.

or start your own business; it's always better if you can spend your working days doing something fulfilling, as long as you're a contributing member of society. Doing what you have a passion for is more important than making tons of money, unless of course your passion is to make tons of money, and that's okay too. Just don't go crazy and worship blindly at the altar of the almighty dollar.

One big stress producer in our wired world is that we're all connected and know about everyone else's lifestyle. We get too stressed about trying to keep up with others and worrying about how they will judge us. Find what gives your life meaning. Be comfortable in your skin. Go forth and live life -- be it as a butcher, baker or candlestick maker. Of course if you're able-bodied and your passion is to sit on your butt, drink beer and do nothing, you're a waste of skin.

Don't Be a Waste of Skin

During World War II, one-third of those in the military were volunteers and two-thirds were drafted into service. During the Korean War half were volunteers and half were drafted. In Vietnam, two-thirds were volunteers and one-third were drafted into service. The draft was eliminated in 1973, and the era of the all-volunteer military began. Some would say this was a good thing since it spared citizens from the rigors of an involuntary military life, but I believe it has had the unintended consequence of turning John Kennedy's famous "...ask not what your country can do for you, ask what you can do for for your country" quote on its head. With so few Americans having any skin-in-the-game by serving their country in any capacity, many now ask, "What can the government do for me?" Most people no longer feel they are part of something bigger than themselves.

In 1994, Oprah Winfrey set out to "destroy the welfare mentality" and started Families For A Better Life, with a goal of moving 100 families out of public housing, off the welfare rolls, and into a life of self-sufficiency within one year. Working with Hull House, a famous Chicago charity serving the needy, the plan was to provide job training, family and financial counseling, health care, and educational assistance to try to break the cycle of poverty. More than 1,600 families applied and were screened to eliminate those with drug or alcohol problems and find people with the "right attitude" and desire to move up in life. After two years and $1.3 million only five families had finished the program, with two of them actually moving out of public housing, so Oprah pulled the plug on the project. When they looked back at the endeavor, one of the reasons cited for its failure was a "mind frame of entitlement" among participants.

Most of the people of the world don't have the opportunities we take for granted. Of the approximately 200 countries in the world I would guess fewer than one third are considered "developed" with free elections, a free press, basic human rights, and all that good stuff. In the grand scheme of things, when you consider that more than three quarters of a billion people don't have access to clean drinking water and about a billion or so don't even have an outhouse and must squat behind a bush to go to the bathroom, this democracy thing we have going is a pretty good gig. If you're reading this book, you're probably one of the lucky ones who has the opportunity and freedom to do just about whatever you want. Take advantage of it.

Without a doubt we have our problems, but so does every family, town, state and nation in the world, developed or otherwise. But if we don't work to preserve what we've got, the party could end. Merely getting a job, paying taxes, voting and saving enough money so you're not a burden on society gives you a good start, and the whole country is better for it. Unfortunately, fewer than 25% of Millennials vote and more and more are looking for the proverbial "free lunch." Should we get to the point where there are more who feel entitled than there are who contribute, it's bad juju. Thomas Jefferson said, "The democracy will cease to exist when you take away from those who are willing to work and give to those who would not."

So, endeavor to be able to look at yourself in the mirror each day and say that you're not a waste of skin, and that you'll be part of the solution and not part of the problem. Do your bit to make the world a better place. And remember to make some memories along the way because when you get older, you'll spend more time regretting the things you didn't do than thinking about the things you did do.

Giving

In May of 2015, the Federal Trade Commission, in collaboration with law enforcement agencies around the country, put several sham cancer charities out of business. James T. Reynolds Sr. of Knoxville, TN and his family used for-profit telemarketing firms to bilk donors out of nearly $190 million running four cancer charities over several decades. Claiming 100% of donated funds were going to cancer patients, they actually spent 97% of the money on luxury cruises, family college tuition, meals at Hooters, lingerie from Victoria's Secret, jet-ski rides and other fun and games. I hope they all have an extended stay in a gated community and get to realize the truth in that old adage: "Fun flies when you're doing time."

I've never been big on just giving money and things to anyone except the most truly needy. Instead I believe educating and training people to stand on their own two feet is a better way (teach a man to fish...). It may cost a little more up front but it's better in the long run. Most of us have an innate desire to help those less fortunate, but not all charitable organizations are created equal, and not all of them are good places to send your hard-earned cash.

There are literally thousands of charities, all wanting your money, so how do you help the needy but not the greedy? A good place to start is at **charitynavigator.org**. Click on Top Ten Lists, then look at some of the less desirable characters such as Low Rated Charities or Inefficient Fundraisers. You'll find charities where, like Mr. Reynolds's scam, very little is actually spent on the services it exists to provide. Now look at some of the better ones like Top Notch Charities or those with the most consecutive four star ratings and you'll see a vast difference. Charity Navigator breaks down expenses to show money spent on programs, fund-raising and administration. Guidelines provided by Independent Sector, a membership organization of non-profits, recommends a minimum of 65% of total expenses be spent on program activities. Sometimes circumstances require more spending on admin costs or fund-raising but any organization spending less than 60% on their cause is a red flag for me.

You obviously get a bigger bang for your buck when donating to a more efficient charity. Charity Navigator only rates those that file IRS Form 990 and have at least $1 million in revenue, so church-based charities such as the Salvation Army and smaller organizations won't be found. If you don't find what you're looking for at Charity Navigator, you can also search the Better Business Bureau's charity website at **give.org** or try the American Institute of Philanthropy website at **charitywatch.org**. Here are a few guidelines to help you in your quest to help others:

1. Never commit to anything, over the phone or in person, before checking it out.
2. Pick a cause you're passionate about then research the charities involved.
3. Give generously over the long haul but check up on the organization periodically.

Giving doesn't have to be just about money. You can also give time. Millennials, and everyone else for that matter, should volunteer in their community. While giving money to your favorite charity allows you to put a check in that "I feel good about myself" box, and might get you a deduction on your tax return, it's not quite the same as getting your hands dirty doing a good deed. A few hours volunteering each month could change your outlook on life.

You might even meet some new and interesting people along the way. Sam was volunteering with the Chamber of Commerce in Americus, Georgia, when a local peanut farmer from nearby Plains, named Jimmy Carter stuck his head in the door to say hello. You can serve food at a shelter, pick up trash, teach someone to read, visit old folks, rock babies at the hospital nursery, coach in a youth league or work in a food pantry. The opportunities and needs are endless. The object is to lend a hand and make the community you live in a better place. Though you may run across someone now and then who's trying to game the system, don't let that keep you from getting the big warm fuzzy you'll find when you give back to your community while expecting nothing in return. And remember, extracurricular activities are a big resume item with potential employers these days.

The Troops Eat First

On a hot Saturday night in the summer of 1953, a drunk and dejected 21-year-old young man sat in the Gilmer County jail in Ellijay, Georgia, knowing he had no one to blame for his sorry situation but himself, and also knowing he had to turn his life around. Soon after, he stepped off of a bus in Paris Island, South Carolina, and the process began. That young man was named Zell Miller, and he went on to become a Marine, a governor, a United States Senator, an author, and much revered in the mountains of north Georgia. One of his many books is called ***Corps Values: Everything You Need to Know I Learned in the Marines***. It was a wonderful reflection on the values he learned in the Corps and how they influenced him throughout life.

One of the core tenets of leadership in the Marine Corps is "the troops eat first." The Sergeant doesn't eat until the squad is fed, the Lieutenant doesn't eat until the platoon is taken care of, the Captain doesn't eat 'til the company has eaten, and so forth up the ranks. Those given the privilege of leading others learn that if you make your needs subservient to those under you, you'll have a team that gives you 110%, especially when the chips are down.

Bestselling author Simon Sinek, in his book **Leaders Eat Last: Why Some Teams Pull Together and Others Don't**, says many overpaid, so-called leaders in business today enjoy the perks and trappings of their position at the expense of their employees, even though their success is due to the labors of those employees. This behavior can often be seen at under-performing companies or those with high turnover rates. Sinek contends that great leaders think, act and communicate differently, and that their success is due to their use of positive reinforcement and the way people respond to it.

If you hire people who just need a job they'll work for your money, but if you can inspire people to buy into your vision, and you treat them right, they'll give you blood, sweat and tears. Sinek says this is because our brains are hard wired to respond to approval of our labors. The brain actually releases neurotransmitters that give the feeling of accomplishment and trust. So if you should ever find yourself in charge of other people, just remember, "the troops eat first." Of course you may run across some outlier who tries to take advantage of you, but for the most part you've got to believe in the fundamental goodness of people and the biology that drives them.

Wild and Crazy Sour Beer – Just about all of the beers produced in the world are lagers or ales but there are some exceptions, the most notable of which are the beers that originated centuries ago with the Trappist monks of Belgium. During the Middle Ages monastery brew-houses were scattered throughout Europe and there are still eleven active today.

Most modern beers are brewed in stainless steel vats using only pure cultures of yeast in a very sterile and controlled environment to keep out bacteria. Not so with Belgian beers. Brewmasters intentionally infect them with wild yeasts and bacteria that gives them a tart, sometimes sour flavor. These top-fermented, high-alcohol brews are then aged for months and often years in large wooden vats called foeders (pronounced food-ers) that impart additional flavor. Since it involves using wild yeasts the process is very unpredictable, and each batch can be different so you'll often find them sold as a "limited release." The most common Belgian beers are Lambic, Flanders red ale and Gueuze. It is said that a good batch might produce a brew that tastes of leather, fruit or smoke and a less successful batch might have a taste somewhere between a horse blanket and a baby diaper. Bon appétit!

There may be such a thing as a natural leader but for most it's a learned skill. While leadership and management go hand in hand, they aren't exactly the same thing. Management is more about organizing and coordinating workers to maximize efficiency, while leadership is about motivating and inspiring people. The leader focuses on people while the manager is concerned about structure and systems. We need both kinds and often one person has to wear both hats. People work for managers but follow leaders.

You Millennials will be taking over the world soon enough, but in the meantime, as you're working your way up the ladder, notice the leadership styles of those you work for. It's been said that imitation is the sincerest form of flattery, so talk to the good ones about their philosophy on leadership and do what they do. And try not to emulate those poor leaders you'll inevitably be stuck working for somewhere along life's path.

Don't Judge A Book By Its Cover

Human nature is a funny thing. When Eastern Airlines went belly up, Pan Am hired a group of former Eastern pilots and sent us to Miami for initial training which proved to be a revealing cultural experience.

Ten years earlier Pan Am, with its big blue-globe logo, had purchased National Airlines with a big orange sun on its tail, and their attempt to integrate two different corporate cultures proved to be a colossal failure. The workforce quickly devolved into a "blue" camp and an "orange" camp with both sides blaming the other for Pan Am's declining fortunes.

But here's where it gets interesting: I was initially based in Miami, which was "orange" territory, and found many of my former Eastern colleagues complaining whenever they had to fly with a "blue" crew from New York. Even though they might have never met the other pilots and knew nothing about them, they automatically didn't like them. When I was transferred to New York, which was "blue" country, it was the same situation except of course my former Eastern colleagues there were carping whenever they had to fly with an "orange" #*@^! (you fill in the blank) from Miami. Many of the former Eastern pilots had developed attitudes about a group of people they had never met, or knew absolutely anything about, based on an event that happened 10 years before we even arrived on the property. Psychologists call these self-fulfilling expectations the Golem Effect, or sometimes the Pygmalion/Golem Effect. You see it a lot in politics and religion, but if you're aware of it, you're less likely to fall for it.

One iconic American author whose stories often delved into human behavior was Doctor

Seuss, and I think his satire on discrimination, titled **The Sneetches**, is one of his best. Sneetches were yellow creatures, and some of them were superior to others because they had green stars on their bellies. Then, along came quick talking salesman Sylvester McMonkey McBean with his Star-on machine, and offered the plain-bellied Sneetches, for a small fee, a chance to put "stars upon thars." Of course this meant the star belly Sneetches were no longer unique, so McBean offered them, for a small fee of course, the use of his Star-off machine so they could once again be different. It was "Off again! On again! In again! Out again!" until all the Sneetches were mixed up and out of money, and Sylvester McMonkey McBean left a rich man, laughing at their folly.

So here's my take-away about human nature: As we saw with the Minnesota Twins, some things like intelligence and personality can be chalked up to genetics, but when it comes to

Dow – Perceptions are as valid as reality, and it's not just blue and orange pilots who are susceptible. One example of this is the story of the Dow Corning Company, a large multinational corporation that manufactured thousands of products including sealants, adhesives, lubricants and silicone. In 1977 a lady sued Dow claiming that her breast implants caused pain and suffering even though they had been used throughout the world for 15 years without incident. Then in 1980, Ralph Nader put out a warning that silicone breast implants caused cancer, and in 1984 a woman sued Dow and won, after convincing a jury the implants caused her autoimmune disease. In 1992, after a television show called "Face to Face with Connie Chung" focused on the supposed dangers of breast implants, the FDA banned their further use, and the legal floodgates were opened. By 1995 there were more than 20,000 individual lawsuits and 410,000 claims as part of a class action lawsuit. Unable to afford the legal costs to defend itself, Dow Corning filed for bankruptcy, and in 1998 agreed to pay $3.2 billion to settle claims. Interestingly, most claims were thrown out by judges.

The reality of this saga is that no other nation in the world removed silicone breast implants from the market, and hundreds of scientific studies around the world (Mayo Clinic, the National Academy of Sciences, American Academy of Neurology, National Cancer Institute among them) failed to find any connection between silicone breast implants and any disease. In 2004 the litigation ended with little media fanfare, and in 2006 the FDA quietly removed its ban.

attitudes about other cultures, religions, politics, the color of someone's skin, or even how you deal with other pilots based on the color of the logo on the airplane they flew, it's much more a learned behavior. Life is too short to get your panties in a twist and waste a lot of brain cells over such matters, so if you just make an effort to limit your preconceived notions, you might learn to look at things from a different perspective, make a few new friends along the way, and hopefully be a better person for it.

Blue Zones

Dinosaurs roamed the planet for 165 million years, but we humans have only been walking upright for around 200,000 years and drinking beer for 7,000 years. That makes us relative newbies in the grand scheme of things. But man, have we made progress! Advances in medicine, science, technology, public health and sanitation have increased our life expectancy from about 30 in 1800, to 47 in 1900, to around 80 today.

Think about this. Of all the people in history who have reached the age of 65, half are alive today. WOW! That's amazing. Now think about this. Despite all of our wonderful

---

Mr. Geisel – Theodor Geisel, the son of German immigrants, grew up in Springfield Mass and enjoyed writing and drawing. He went to Dartmouth College in 1921, and by his senior year was editor of *Jack-O-Lantern*, the school's humor magazine. Life was good until Dean Craven Laycock caught Geisel and his friends drinking bootleg gin in his dorm room, and banned Geisel from extracurricular activities for violating prohibition laws. Not to be outdone, Geisel continued writing using such pen names as L. Pasteur, D. G. Rossetti, Seuss (his middle name and his mother's maiden name), T. Seuss, and Dr. Theophrastus Seuss, which was eventually shortened to Dr. Seuss.

Later in life he would write, but not illustrate, 13 books as Theo LeSieg, which is Geisel spelled backwards. In 1975, he and friend Mike Firth published ***Because a Little Bug Went Ka-Choo*** using the nom-de-plume Rosetta Stone, which was Geisel's wife's maiden name. Although the family name was pronounced "zoice" (rhymes with voice), once he became famous, most Americans anglicanized the pronunciation to "soose" and the author went with it.

In 1918, young Theodor was one of ten Boy Scouts slated to receive a medal from former President Teddy Roosevelt for selling War Bonds. Theo was last in line and TR was only given nine medals to hand out. When the tenth Scout walked on stage TR boomed; "What's this boy doing here?" Geisel was so traumatized that for the rest of his life he had a phobia of speaking before large crowds.

technological and scientific advances, Millennials run the risk of being the first generation in history whose life expectancy is less than that of their parents. Double WOW! While the progress of science has been moving at warp speed, the pace of human evolution creeps along like a snail and can't keep up. Our bodies adapt much slower than this rapid technological change so we have to continue to do some things our ancestors have been doing for millennia. Sometimes it pays to look backward to see the way forward.

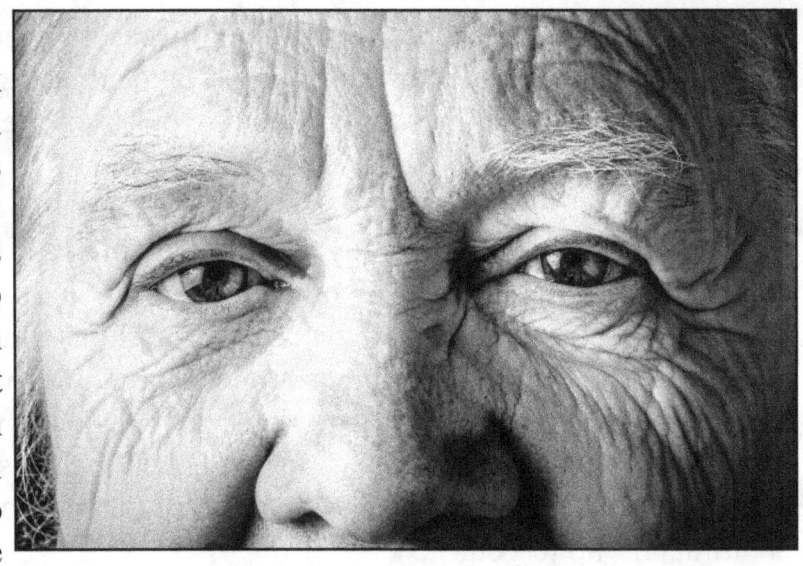

If you live to 100 in any culture, you've hit the genetic lottery. In 2000, as he was studying long-lived people in Sardinia, Belgian researcher Dr. Michel Poulain used blue ink to circle the villages on his map with unusual numbers of centurions, giving rise to the term Blue Zones. Demographers soon found other Blue Zones in the world where large numbers of people lived to triple digits, including remote areas of Okinawa, Costa Rica, Greece, and of all places, Loma Linda, California, which is home to a large Seventh Day Adventist community that encourages a healthy diet and lifestyle.

So, what can Millennials learn from these seniors to help navigate today's world? The typical 100 + year old Blue Zone person lives a simple life, eats a mostly plant based diet, has strong family and social networks, gets moderate exercise daily, usually by walking or gardening, and has a strong sense of purpose and a positive attitude about life. Some drink wine every day (Sardinia and Greece) while others abstain from alcohol and drink mostly water (Loma Linda, Okinawa and Costa Rica). Except for Loma Linda, Blue Zones are somewhat culturally isolated, so they haven't been exposed to the full negative effects of modern society.

Science tells us that only about 25% of how long we live is determined by genes and the rest is a function of lifestyle choices that we make. An overwhelming majority of cancers for instance, (some studies say up to 90%) are caused by diet, lifestyle and the environment, not genes. There are more deaths worldwide from preventable, non-communicable diseases than all other diseases combined. We are literally killing ourselves! While the average body should last about 90 years, we Americans have a life expectancy of around 80, while the folks in Blue Zones live way beyond that and are generally free of heart disease, hypertension, diabetes, obesity and other diseases. There's a lesson here for all of us when it comes to health, and that is we should take advantage of all that modern medicine has to offer, but when it comes to how we live our lives there's a lot to be learned from the old ways.

It may help to think of your body as akin to owning a house. When you own a house you're responsible for the upkeep so you change a light bulb, fix the leaking faucet, or do some painting. But sometimes it's beyond your abilities and you need to call on professional help, maybe a carpenter, plumber or electrician. It's the same thing with the body you've been given to live in, except you don't get to choose what kind of body you're given at birth, but you do have a lot to do with the final design and how long it lasts. While sometimes you may need professional help – nurses, doctors, dentists – the overall upkeep is ultimately up to you.

We had a rescue dog named Mia who was part of our family for sixteen years. Although her hearing went as she got older, for the most part she was healthy up until the last few

> **Germ Theory** – Freddie Freeman is an all-star first baseman for the Atlanta Braves. Whenever a teammate scores, he gives him a hug. Other players high five, fist bump, or even throw dirt on one another, but not Freddie -- he gives hugs. And that's a wonderful thing because mammals, and we are mammals, crave tactile contact. For newborn babies it's required for survival.
>
> In the 19th century, in what became known as "germ theory," scientists like Pasteur, Lister and Koch posited that disease was caused by microorganisms too small to be seen except through a microscope. By 1915 researchers noted that large numbers of babies in orphanages around the world were dying within the first year as a result of "mesmarus" (Greek for "wasting away"), and those who survived often suffered severe mental and physical problems. Relying on germ theory, many orphanages thought it best to keep infants in as sterile an environment as possible which resulted in minimal tactile stimulation for the babies. For the most part, the only human contact the infants received was for feeding, changing and occasional bathing. Then it was discovered that at orphanages where babies were held on a regular basis, death rates plummeted. The magic bullet was mere skin-to-skin touching, which it turns out, stimulates growth hormones in the brain and development of the immune system. This isn't just a human phenomenon, it applies to all mammals, from rats, to pigs, to monkeys. While reptiles can lay their eggs and leave, we mammals must birth, nurture and raise our young to complete an "external gestation" period, and touch is a very big part of that. So, be like Freddie and give those you love a hug every now and then.

months of her life. We should all be so lucky. It's better to live a vibrant life till the end instead of a decades long decline filled with chronic problems. The Blue Zoners can show us the way. Basically we need to move, eat better and learn how to chill. So now is the time to start taking responsibility for your health and live like Mia the wonder dog.

Move!

As we went from living in caves, to being nomadic hunter-gatherers, to urbanizing in communities, we were always physically active. Even when the The Industrial Revolutions brought machines to make us more productive, we still labored in the fields, toiled in the factories and exerted physical energy. And then it happened. Wham! The Modern Age, the Internet Revolution, the entire world just a click away. We could accomplish unimaginable things without leaving our chairs, but unfortunately, as the Blue Zoners showed us, this progress has had its downside.

Pretty much everyone these days would agree that smoking is bad for you, but Dr. James Levine of the Mayo Clinic argues that sitting is even worse than smoking when it comes to health in the developed world. In the 1960s about half of all jobs required some measure of physical activity, but today 80% of jobs are sedentary. In his book ***Get Up! Why Your Chair is Killing You and What You Can Do About It***, he says the average American now sits 13 hours a day (plus 8 hours sleeping and 3 hours moving) and explains that we were not structurally designed to spend that amount of time on our rumps. Levine has spent the last 25 years in his Non-Exercise Activity Thermogenesis (NEAT) laboratory studying the effects of a sedentary lifestyle and found that excessive sitting contributes to increased rates of obesity, diabetes, heart disease, cancer, and depression. One Australian study even showed that for every hour spent sitting we decrease our lifespan by 22 minutes.

Moving is not the same as exercise so don't confuse the two. If you're part of the 15% among us who are gym rats and regularly work out, be it a spin class, lifting weights or Pilates, you should know that while it does help your cardiovascular system, muscle tone and burns a few calories, it does very little to reverse the negative effects of prolonged sitting. To counter the effects of sitting 13 hours a day, you've got to not sit 13 hours a day. It's that simple. There's no single magic number of hours that you must stay off your backside but the fewer the better. One large study showed that people who sat for 11 hours a day had a 40% greater risk of premature death than those who sat for four hours.

Walking, even at one mile an hour, is far superior to sitting, and in this regard technology may come to the rescue. Today the clip-on-your-belt old style pedometer for counting your steps has given way to a host of apps for smart phones or wearable fitness trackers (Gruve, Fitbit, miCoach) that count your steps and do a whole lot more. These are great little gizmos that provide instant feedback and allow you to track your progress. If you try one, set a goal of getting 10,000 steps a day (some doctors now say 7,000 steps are all that are needed) be it by walking, gardening, cooking, bird-watching or whatever. Any kind of movement is better than the killer chair.

Here's an example of the profound effect moving can have on the body. After eating a meal, your blood sugar peaks, causing a release of insulin (more on that later). If the sugar is not used, it hangs around for hours in your bloodstream, and if this happens too often, your body can become less sensitive to the high levels of insulin and develop high blood sugar (prediabetes) and eventually diabetes. But if you take a slow 15 minute stroll after eating, what the Italians call passeggiata, your blood sugar levels are halved because your muscles, especially the large muscles in your legs, are using glucose.

Levine took his own research to heart, and in 2000 cobbled together a desk from broken furniture and placed it over a treadmill he modified, to create the first treadmill desk. Today more than 50,000 are in use. If you had one at work and set the pace at one mile per hour, which is barely moving, by the end of the day you would have walked eight miles, like a Blue Zone native. If a treadmill desk won't work for you, try a standing desk (Charles Dickens and Thomas Jefferson used them), which studies show increase productivity by about ten percent. You can build your own just by using a high table instead of a traditional desk or putting your computer on a box or stacks of books to elevate it. Some researchers say it's not a completely natural transition and usually takes about two weeks to get used to standing. If you don't walk or stand while working, at the very least get up from your killer chair and walk around for ten minutes every hour, take the stairs instead of the elevator if you're only going a couple floors and squeeze in a short walk after lunch.

Eat

More than 2,400 years ago Hippocrates said "Let food be thy medicine." Smart man that Hippocrates. (I wonder if his friends called him Hippo.) Today we're faced with the Standard American Diet (SAD) which is in fact, pretty sad, and we have no one to blame but ourselves because we've come to put speed and convenience above everything else.

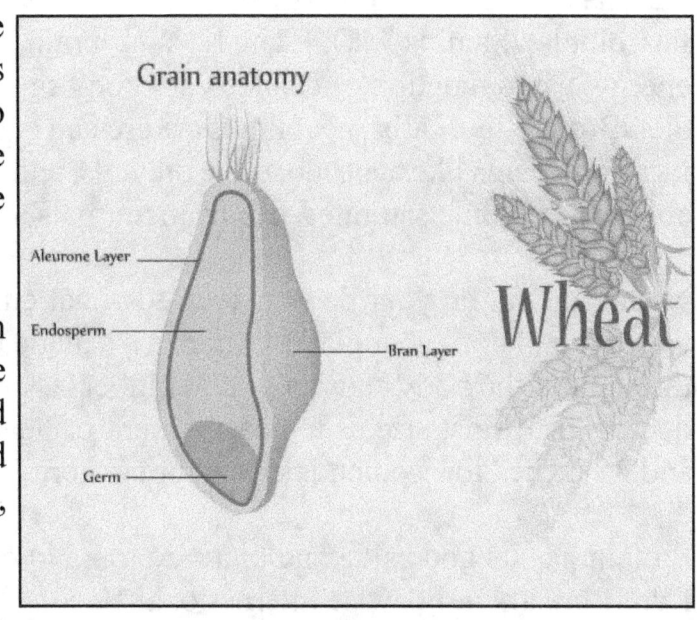

This is not a diet book, but for your own health you need to keep a few big picture things in mind about carbs, fats and protein. There are good carbohydrates and bad carbohydrates, good fats and bad fats, and good proteins and bad proteins.

First let's talk carbs. Grains like wheat, corn, rice, rye, oats, and barley consist of three layers, a fiber-rich outer layer called bran, a middle part called the endosperm, and a nutrient-rich inner part called the germ. When you eat carbs your body converts them into glucose for energy, and the pancreas pumps out insulin to get the glucose into your cells. With complex whole carbs, which include the bran and germ, it takes the body longer to break them down, so the glucose is released slowly into the bloodstream and lesser amounts of insulin are required to handle it. But when you eat simple carbs, where the bran and germ have been removed by refining, it creates an insulin spike to do the job. That's bad news and over time wreaks havoc with your body. Fruits and veggies are also simple carbs but they contain fiber which slows their digestion so they act more like complex carbs, that's why eating a piece of whole fruit is kinder to your pancreas than drinking fruit juice. Refined carbs, such as sugar, soda, candy, and enriched bread, pastas and rice are really hard on the system and cause a huge spike in insulin.

In addition to eating too many of the wrong kind of carbs, we are eating way too many of them. Carbs now make up 60% to 70% of the average American's sad diet. It would be better to limit them to around 50% and stick with whole grains, veggies and fruit. One last thing about carbs: When manufacturers refine grains and remove the bran and germ, and thereby most of the nutrition, they add back some vitamins and call it "enriched." Read the labels and don't be fooled, if for example you're buying a loaf of brown bread and it says enriched flour, it is not whole wheat, it's just brown.

Fats have been given a bad rap. Your body needs fats to function and to absorb the fat-soluble vitamins A, D, E and K. Your brain is 60% fat and consumes 20% of the body's energy just to function, and since your body can't produce fat you need to include it in your diet. But just like carbs, not all fats are created equal. The essential fatty acids in unsaturated fats from plants like avocado, olive oil, nuts, and fish like salmon, cod, herring and sardines, are the best while saturated fats from animals are the worst.

Not all the fat on your body is created equal either. The visceral fat around your belly is worse than fat in other places because it's made up of molecules that trigger inflammation throughout the body and put you at higher risk of heart disease and diabetes. That is why doctors use waist size as a measurement of health risk -- greater than 40 inches for men and 35 inches for women is cause for concern.

Protein has its good side and bad side too. No one likes bacon wrapped bacon more than I do. I breathlessly await International Bacon Day (the Saturday before Labor Day) like Linus awaits the Great Pumpkin. So it saddens me to report that the long-running Chick-fil-A ad campaign encouraging us to *Eat Mor Chikin*, has some hard science behind it. The International Agency for Research on Cancer, after doing meta-analysis of more than 800 studies, says that red meat (beef, pork, lamb, goat, and horse) and processed meat of any color, are linked to cancer. Stomach, prostate, and pancreatic cancers are all

> **Brewski** – According to *The Huffington Post* beer is unfairly left out of the conversation when it comes to the health benefits of alcohol. Everyone knows that a glass or two of wine every day is supposed to be part of a healthy diet and reduces your risk of heart disease by 31%. But so does beer. Plus moderate beer consumption reduces the risk of kidney stones by 41%, and thanks to the the hops and barley, is a source of phytonutrients. The yeast used in the brewing process also provides some vitamin B-12, and brews such as Guiness Stout, which the Irish refer to as "liquid bread," provide fiber. It's beginning to sound like the near perfect food to me. So let's toast the "nectar fit for the gods" and remember what they used to say back in the day, "I'd rather have a bottle in front of me, than a frontal lobotomy." Here, here!

influenced by red and processed meat consumption but the connection to colorectal cancer is compelling.

The culprit in processed meats is the nitrates used to preserve them. When they get into your body they form carcinogenic nitrosamines which can damage DNA. With red meats there's a rascal called heme iron (plants contain nonheme iron) which bonds with a molecule called protoporphyrin and can wreak havoc on cells in the large bowel, and if you cook any meat at high temperatures it creates chemicals (PAHs and HCAs) that can also damage DNA. Your risk of colorectal cancer increases by 18% if you eat 50 grams of processed meat a day -- that's one hot dog, five slices of hard salami, or six slices of bacon. The only good news in this story is that our annual consumption of red meat is now down to 71 pounds per capita, from 96 pounds in 1970, and colorectal cancer rates have fallen accordingly.

Vegetarians typically drink less alcohol, smoke less, and are more physically active than their meat eating peers, so one might assume they are healthier as a group. Being an equal opportunity food critic, I have to point out that a recent study from the Medical University of Graz in Austria shows that vegetarians suffer significantly more chronic illnesses. They have higher rates of allergies, asthma, osteoporosis, and migraines, and are twice as likely to suffer from depression and anxiety. So what is one to make of all this confusing data? I think it's wise to eat fewer four-legged critters and more with fins and feathers, and slow down on the processed carbs and junk snacks. And I'm convinced that what Hippocrates taught two

Liquid Gold? – In 1879 chemist Joseph Lawrence developed an alcohol-based germicide and called it Listerine in honor of Joseph Lister, the father of antiseptic surgery. (It was reportedly also good for cleaning floors.) By 1895 it was being pitched to dentists for oral care and became the first over-the-counter mouthwash sold in the US.

Original Listerine was yellow in color and tasted terrible, and I've often wondered if that was inspired by the ancient Roman's use of urine as a mouthwash. Urine is a rich source of urea and over time decays into ammonia which the Romans prized for tanning animal hides, cleaning laundry (whiter whites and brighter colors), and yes, even mouthwash. Particularly prized was urine from Portugal, so popular in fact that Nero put a tax on it, as he did with pee from all public urinals. Kind of makes you wince, doesn't it.

thousand years ago still applies today: everything in moderation.

When Grandma said "Eat your veggies," she knew what she was talking about. To function properly our bods require thirteen vitamins and a host of minerals, and you can get just about all you need if you eat a balanced diet. The problem is, a lot of us don't eat a balanced diet and think we can just pop a vitamin pill and go on eating our SAD food. Nothing could be farther from the truth. While that pill might provide some vitamins and minerals, it does nothing when it comes to phytonutrients. Phyto means plant based, and more than a thousand of these chemicals, which are used by the body to protect us from disease, have been identified. They're spread out among veggies, fruits, beans, grains, and beverages derived from plants such as tea, wine, and beer. It's why there is no one best or perfect food. You need variety. The most nutrient dense foods for phytonutrients are dark green leafy veggies, followed by other green veggies, non-green non-starchy veggies, fresh fruit, legumes, starchy veggies, whole grains and fish.

We Americans do everything in a big way: big houses, big cars, big plates, big bowls, big glasses, big meals, big everything. Brian Wansink, author of **Mindless Eating**, studied the size of various containers of food and compared them to how much we consume and found that the larger the container, the more we ate. In one study he gave subjects a tape to watch and either a half pound or one pound bag of M&Ms. As expected, the people with the half pound bag ate 63 M&Ms while those with the one pound bag ate 120. He repeated this with many other foods and the results were always the same.

To see if this was because of a clean-your-plate mentality, Wansink gave people either a medium or large box of spaghetti to fix a meal and of course, those who got the bigger box ate more. The kicker was that he had removed half of the spaghetti from the larger box so that both boxes had the same amount in them.

The design of the packaging also has a big influence on our eating behavior, as does the description of the food. Subjects given "Chocolate Cake" said it was "okay," and they were "not very likely" to order it again. Those given "Belgian Black Forest Double Chocolate Cake" said "...that was pretty good, I like the taste," and that they'd likely order it again, even though both slices were from the same cake. Here are a few more tidbits from Dr. Wansink's research:

– People eat 22% less when changing from a 12" plate to a 10" plate;
– Healthy sounding labels like "low fat" lead people to consume 20% more calories;
– People will pour 26% more, (and therefor consume more) into a short wide glass than a tall skinny one.

The problem is not only the food we eat and how much we consume, but also our relationship with food itself. Have you ever seen someone down a one pound burrito, in ten minutes and chase it with a 20 ounce soda, all while standing? In France they eat a rich, high fat diet yet have lower rates of obesity and heart disease than we have. There aren't any Blue Zones in France, but they do have a lot in common with the long-lived peoples of the world when it comes to eating. While we Americans eat 'til we're full, in the Blue Zones of Okinawa for example, they eat 'til they're not hungry.

The French have a totally different mindset than us when it comes to eating. They have smaller portions but take much longer to eat them, because eating is meant to be a pleasurable social experience where food is to be savored, not the usual 30-minute American pig-out we engage in while watching television, multitasking or, God forbid, standing. The French usually go for quality and freshness over quantity, and the longer time they take to enjoy their meal actually means they eat less, because it takes about twenty minutes for your food to "hit bottom" and signal your brain that you're full. So the next time you're so hungry you could gnaw the hump off a camel, just remember to slow down and savor that first helping and you'll be less likely to rush for a second.

Basically, we're eating too many of the wrong fats and proteins, and we're carb-loading like marathoners before a race, except we're not running. We're not even walking - we're sitting! The sad thing is that too many Millennials are taking this to a whole new level. But you can change. You don't have to move to Sardinia and herd goats to live longer. Just use some common sense when it comes to your health. So get your head out of the sand

> **Jorge** – My friend Jorge is an executive with a large corporation and needed to lose some weight. Instead of going on a strict diet he decided to simply modify his lifestyle. He didn't move to Sardinia to herd goats but did give up most processed and refined foods and switched to fresh foods. And he walked just about every day. No diet, no calorie counting, no portion control, just lots of fresh food. While Jorge still ate his meat and fish and continued to drink beer, over the course of a year he lost sixty pounds. Muy bueno, Jorge!

and make a resolution to begin changing the way you eat. Remember, denial is not a river in Africa.

Chill

Go back 12,000 years and our ancestors had occasional stress from natural disasters, famine or perhaps being treed by a saber-tooth cat. Today stress is everywhere. Sometimes a little bit of stress can be a good thing. When you have a job interview or deadline for a project it can help increase your focus. But over time, repeated stress can take a toll on your immune system and make you more susceptible to infections and other conditions. The body's biological reaction to stress is inflammation, whether it comes from anxiety, infection or physical injury. Extended mental stress, so common in our fast-paced, wired world, leads to chronic inflammation, which is bad juju and is a player in a host of medical conditions including auto-immune diseases, allergies, cancer, Alzheimer's, anxiety and depression. You can be cruising through life fat, dumb, and happy and not even realize the effect stress is having on your body because stress is cumulative and it's sneaky.

It's kind of like doing tequila shooters. Everything is going just fine, and then after four or five shots, *wham*, Señor Tequila creeps up behind you and hits you up side of the head with a 2 by 4.

Scientists have been trying to predict and quantify the effects of stress for decades and over the years they have developed self-scoring questionnaires to do this. There are dozens of these self-assessment scales designed for children, teens, college students, the elderly and others but the most famous is the *Social Readjustment Rating Scale* by T. H. Homes and T. H. Rahe. (see Dr. Rahe's website is **www.drrahe.com**) which shows the relationship between stress and illness. Additional research shows that these tests can also be a good predictor of having an accident. It's rather obvious that horrendous events like the death of a family member, or divorce would rate high on any scale measuring stress. But what you probably didn't realize is that even good things like vacation, moving, beginning school, graduating, and holidays can be stressful.

On the following Social Rating Scale chart, mark all that apply to you and total your points. You'll notice that all the items on the scale deal with change, and since the ability to cope with change varies from person to person, interpreting your score is inexact, but here are some ballpark guidelines: A score less than 150 is good. If you have 150 to 299 points, statistically you have a 50% chance of getting sick in the near future. If your total is 300 or more, you're looking at an 80% chance.

A lot of stress is self-generated. Let's say you're driving down the highway and some turd-head speeds by and cuts you off. You have a decision to make. You can flip him the bird, step on the gas and get even, which will increase your pulse, blood pressure, breathing and promote inflammation. That's a lose-lose decision that often turns out poorly. Or you can give the other driver the benefit of the doubt and assume he's rushing home because of a family emergency which eliminates all the physical symptoms. Of course, if that driver laughs and flips you the bird as he's cutting you off, then he is a turd-head, but you still don't have to get your panties in a twist. Just chuckle to yourself knowing that he's an accident looking for a place to happen as you call 911 with his tag number. With practice you can train yourself to think positive.

Another thing you can do to reduce stress is to be happy. No one is predetermined to be sad or happy and it's usually a choice we make. It's easy to be unhappy, but you sometimes have to work at being happy. Happiness is uniquely human - animals just want to be free from pain and sated - and some argue that it's a moral obligation that each of us should work on because nobody likes to be around a Debbie Downer.

Esteemed family physician William Snell of Marietta, Georgia, sends weekly emails to his

Life Event	Life Change Units
Death of a spouse	100
Divorce	73
Marital separation	65
Imprisonment	63
Death of a close family member	63
Personal injury or illness	53
Marriage	50
Dismissal from work	47
Marital reconciliation	45
Retirement	45
Change in health of family member	44
Pregnancy	40
Sexual difficulties	39
Gain a new family member	39
Business readjustment	39
Change in financial state	38
Death of a close friend	37
Change to different line of work	36
Change in frequency of arguments	35
Major mortgage	32
Foreclosure of mortgage or loan	30
Change in responsibilities at work	29
Child leaving home	29
Trouble with in-laws	29
Outstanding personal achievement	28
Spouse starts or stops work	26
Begin or end school	26
Change in living conditions	25
Revision of personal habits	24
Trouble with boss	23
Change in working hours or conditions	20
Change in residence	20
Change in schools	20
Change in recreation	19
Change in church activities	19
Change in social activities	18
Minor mortgage or loan	17
Change in sleeping habits	16
Change in number of family reunions	15
Change in eating habits	15
Vacation	13
Christmas	12
Minor violation of law	11

patients in a proactive effort to educate and encourage them to take more responsibility for their own well-being. Dr. Snell sent one about happiness and its effects on our health. He said Mayo Clinic research shows that only a small portion of our happiness is due to our circumstances. Most of it is because of our choices, thoughts, behavior and personality.

Beware of letting society define happiness for you. Contrary to what you see on the idiot tube, being rich and beautiful is no guarantee of happiness. Mayo says those people are no happier than the rest of us. Being happy is good for your health and provides for better immune function and lower stress. Plus, happy people live longer. Smiling, laughing, doing altruistic works, exercise, finding purpose in life, meditating, having happy friends, acceptance of who you are, and expressing gratitude all bring us joy. And the best part is that happiness is free and can be contagious. Happiness is purely subjective and different for everyone. One person might find happiness out fishing by themselves or sitting alone by the fire reading a good book while another might find it among a crowd of friends. So practice being happy every chance you get.

Happiness is such a big deal that in 2012, in recognition of the importance of happiness and well-being, the United Nations General Assembly passed a resolution proclaiming 20 March as the International Day of Happiness. So if I don't see you in March, happy Happiness Day.

be happy Always be aware of Señor Stress and keep an eye out for him.

Jeanne Louise Calment – The oldest verifiable living human of all time was Jeanne Louise Calment of Arles, France who lived to the age of 122 years and 164 days. Born in 1875, the year before Bell invented the telephone, she knew Vincent Van Gogh, saw the Eiffel Tower being built, and outlived her husband, her only child and grandchild. Calment took fencing lessons at age 85, rode a bicycle till she was 100, walked till fracturing her hip at age 114, and attributed her longevity to olive oil, port (wine), laughter, and chocolate. Researchers said she seemed to be immune to stress.

In 1965, having no heirs, at age 90 Calment signed a deal to sell her apartment to a man named Raffray on a contingency contract. He would pay her 2,500 francs (about $500) each month until she died, then he would get the apartment. Of course, she out-lived Raffray, and his widow continued the payments till 1997, when Calment passed away after having received more than 900,000 francs ($180,000), three times the apartment's value. Good for her!

And remember, just because the word "stressed" is "desserts" backwards, doesn't mean it's something you want a lot of in your life.

Head Games

For a long time Captain Jean-Luc Picard has been telling Trekkies that space is the final frontier. That may be true in the not too distant future, but for now I believe the space between our ears fits the bill. Neuroscience research has been exploding, and in recent years we've begun to learn about the effects the wired world is having on our brains. (The average adult is now using media almost eleven hours a day.) Computers and smart phones are wonderful devices but they can, if not used properly, literally take over your life. Using MRI scans, researchers have found actual structural changes in the brains of heavy gamers and surfers. Going back to the nature/nurture debate we talked about in Part I, we know there are many things hard-wired into our brains, but external forces also play a large role in neural development.

Millennials, especially the younger ones, are joined at the hip -- or should I say head -- with the wired world, and it looks like it's going to be even worse for Generation Z. Therapists are seeing greater numbers of cases of internet addiction disorder, (also called problematic internet use, compulsive internet use, or pathological internet use) an impulse control disorder that's similar to gambling disorder and can be as hard to kick as drug addiction. This can have negative consequences on your life including anxiety, lower self-esteem, depression, academic failure, and even marital and financial problems.

Professor Kimberly Young of St. Bonaventure University is an internationally recognized expert and pioneer in the study of internet addiction and has developed an Internet Addiction Test. You can go to her website at **http://netaddiction.com/internet-addiction-test/** and take the test to see where you stand. It only takes a few minutes. Basically she's quantifying the impact the web has on your life. Ask yourself this: Do you have a phone or tablet next to the bed when you sleep, or take one with you when you shower? Do you spend a lot of time typing with your thumbs, hanging onto a game controller, or communicating with acronyms in 140 characters or less? Do you suffer from FOMO (fear of missing out)? You may need help. The good news is that unlike alcoholism and gambling addition where abstinence is required, simply controlling use is the goal for the pathological internet user.

Try this experiment: Turn off all your devices when you go to bed. This might take a little getting used to, and it may even raise your anxiety level when you begin since 80% of Millennials sleep with their cellphone or tablet next to the bed, but give it a try. Then go hog wild and unplug for 24 hours and see if you have withdrawal symptoms. Finally, go for a 48 hour detox. This is not to send you back to the Stone Age, but to prove to yourself that you are the master of that little device in your hand, instead of the other way around.

Dr. Young's research not only looks into how much digital exposure is too much, but also how young is too young. Today we have iPad bouncy seats and iPotty chairs which are causing reading deficits and difficulties with social adjustment as babies get older.

Shrinks are still debating whether this is a true addiction or an obsessive-compulsive disorder or impulse-control disorder, but whatever they finally decide, it's a growing problem that you need to be aware of.

Heilicopters

There have always been "helicopter parents" hovering over their children watching their every move. When General Douglas McArthur went off to West Point in 1899, his mother, Pinky McArthur, went with him. She got a suite at Craney's Hotel from which she could see her son's dorm room to make sure he was studying. He graduated first in his class with no demerits.

It appears that some parents of Millennials have taken things to new heights, especially among the affluent, according to former Stanford Dean Julie Lythcott-Haimes, author of **How To Raise an Adult: Break Free of the Overparenting Trap and Prepare Your Kid for Success**. While Boomers' parents often sent their kids out to play and told them to be back in time for dinner, not knowing where they were going or who they were with, Lythcott-Haimes says modern "helicopter parents" are over-helping their kids and robbing them of the chance to learn how to become self-sufficient and thrive on their own. This has led to an increase in depression, anxiety and other mental health problems. It's great to like and be friends with your parents, but if you find they're calling you several times a day,

---

Break the Seal – We've all experienced this. You're drinking beer while watching the ballgame, and after three or four brews you have to pee. After that it seems the flood gates have opened and you need to go every ten minutes. What gives? Here's the story. Your body doesn't know when it's going to get its next drink so the brain cranks out an anti-diuretic hormone (ADH) called arginine vasopressin to conserve water. Unfortunately alcohol inhibits ADH which turns on the waterworks. Any alcoholic drink can cause this but carbonated ones seem to do a little better job of it.

wanting to help with your homework or be your "mouthpiece" when it comes to interacting with adults in authority, it's time to loosen that parental tether and sally forth on your own. Gently let them know that the training wheels are off and you'll be just fine. And remember that it's okay to stumble or even fail. It's all part of growing up and you'll be a better person for it.

Assume You've Been Hacked

Me explaining anything about computers to a Millennial is like Orville and Wilbur explaining aerodynamics to a Boeing engineer today. People born in the computer age, who grew up with the internet are referred to by those in education and business as "natives," while those who were not born into the digital world are called "immigrants." All but the oldest Millennials are natives, and I am quite definitely an immigrant, but that said, there are some things that even you natives screw up in the digital world.

Twenty years ago cybersecurity meant dealing with mischievous teenagers; ten years ago it involved fighting organized and unorganized criminals; and today we're dealing with sophisticated nation-states, some of whom conspire with organized criminals. Cybercrime is skyrocketing, and identity theft has been the leading complaint reported to the Federal Trade Commission for many years.

The ever-creative bad guys have put a unique twist on plain old identity theft. It's called synthetic ID fraud and is a multi-billion dollar business. The crooks combine real and bogus

> **Notre Dame vs Navy** – Due to a shortage of students during World War II, the all-male University of Notre Dame faced severe financial difficulties and its ability to stay open was in question. The US Navy came to the rescue and established a Navy College Training Program at the school which provided enough cash to keep the doors open, and in thanks, Notre Dame extended an open invitation to play Navy in football. The agreement, which was done on a handshake, is considered by Notre Dame to be payment on a debt of honor, and the historic game is still played today, with Notre Dame hosting in odd years and Navy hosting in even years. Though the results are lopsided in Notre Dame's favor, the contest is still watched by millions and noted for the mutual respect on both sides – each team stands at attention for the singing of the other school's alma mater song – and is scheduled to continue indefinitely.

information to create a fake identity. They might steal one person's social security number and combine it with another person's name and a fake address. Highly prized are social security numbers of children, whose credit might not be checked until they're adults. They then open multiple credit accounts, build up a credit profile, and max the cards out buying gift cards. Then they disappear.

What it boils down to is that we are all pawns among some really big and very sophisticated players. But there are still a few things you can do to protect your personal accounts.

One is to freeze your credit. Freezing your credit is easy to do and prevents anyone from accessing your credit report and thereby opening credit in your name. When you initiate a credit freeze (also called a security freeze) with the credit agencies you will be issued a PIN to be used in case you ever need to "thaw" your account. One word of warning: Put the PIN in a safe place and never lose it, otherwise you may have a difficult time convincing them it's really you, should you need to thaw your credit to make a major purchase. There may be a fee to freeze your credit depending on your age and state of residence, but you can still check your own report at no cost when it's frozen. If you want to open a new account or apply for new credit, you will have to thaw and then refreeze it.

You must do a credit freeze with each of the three credit reporting agencies individually and can begin at the following websites:

Equifax - **www.freeze.equifax.com** or call 800.685.1111
Experian - **www.experian.com/freeze** or call 888.397.3742
Transunion – **https://freeze.transunion.com** or call 888.909.8872

If you have children and you're concerned about someone stealing their identity, there's also information about freezing a minor's credit at each of the websites.

When it comes to passwords I really shouldn't have to tell you to skip the most common ones which are things like *12345* and *password,* yet they're the most common because so many people still use them. And don't use your pet's name, or anyone's name for that matter, or a single word. Keep it simple, so you won't have to write it down, at least eight characters long and use letters, numbers and symbols. Here are a few ideas but use your imagination to create your own. Phrases, like "I ate 17 eggs" (Iate17eggs) or the first letter of each word in a phrase or lyric such as "You are my sunshine, my only sunshine" (Yams,mos) are simple and secure. Or you can customize passwords for different institutions such as "National bank owes me $100" (Nbom$100) and "I love shopping at Bill's Sporting Goods" (IlsaBSG), or substitute symbols for words such as @ for "at" or & for "and." Or try stringing together four to five unrelated words, such as correct, horse, battery, and staple which is remarkably secure — especially if you put capital letters and special characters in unusual places. For example, you could string together trombone, quiz, cathedral, leopard and balm to form a secure password: tromboNequizcaThedralle0pardbAlm. Check out this comic that explains in more detail why this is so secure: **https://xkcd.com/936/**.

Should you find that your identity has been compromised there are places to go for help. The Identity Theft Resource Center is a non-profit organization founded in 1999 to educate and provide victims with assistance, and can be reached at 888.400.5530 or **idtheftcenter.org**. They also provide a lot of good information about scams and data breaches. The Federal Trade Commission website at **identitytheft.gov** provides useful checklists for victims and even covers special situations including tax returns, medical records and child identity theft. Become familiar with both these resources before you need them. Grab a root beer or glass of grape juice and spend an hour or so perusing their websites.

As the Internet-of-Things progresses, more and more things are interconnected and can be accessed remotely. Now we can lock our doors, turn out the lights and set the thermostat from our smart-phones. "Pretty cool" is what I thought at first. But then I got to thinking about it. MySpace, LinkedIn, J. P. Morgan, Target, Anthem Health Insurance, Home Depot, Ebay and others have been hacked, and the personal records of more than four million U. S. government employees were stolen by Chinese hackers. And they're just the ones we know about. I figured maybe bio-metrics would be the answer: then I saw that nearly six million fingerprint records were also stolen from the federal government. Smart-phones, drones, cars with push-button start, driver-less cars, and medical devices like insulin pumps and pacemakers, have all been hacked. When internet service company Dyn was hacked the vulnerability of the Internet-of-Things was exposed as hundreds of thousands of internet connected things such as web-cams, home routers, and baby monitors were infected with malware. The attack effected thousands of web sites including Twitter, Netflix, Spotify, Reddit, Etsy, the New York Times and CNN. Do I really want door locks and an alarm system that can be accessed remotely? Pardon my skepticism, but this immigrant is just not quite ready to jump into the Internet-of-Things until it gets a little more secure. But then again, I'm not a Millennial.

Zombie Apocalypse

Cybersecurity is not the only thing to worry about these days. For more than 100 years the Scout motto has been "Be Prepared," and it's a motto we all should follow. Why is it that every time the weatherman says a bad storm is coming, the stores are clogged with people scrambling to buy bread, candles, baby food, batteries and beer? Just as most of us are poorly prepared for a financial crisis by not having an emergency fund, we are also ill-prepared for even the mildest of natural or man-made disasters. I'm not talking the Zombie Apocalypse here, just a run-of-the-mill 24-hour storm. Most Millennials would stock up on beer, then when the power goes out, organize a beer pong tournament to drink the beer before it gets warm. The next morning you're hungover, and your mouth tastes like the Russian Army marched across your tongue, but the power comes back on and all is well.

But what if it were a Zombie Apocalypse and the power didn't come back on? FEMA says we all should have an evacuation plan, a three day supply of food and water for every person in the house, and the ability to shelter-in-place when needed. It's been said that any society is but 72 hours from anarchy without electricity, running water, police, fire, medical services, and all the other trappings of a modern society. What would you do if the power grid went down? How would you handle severely limited food (no refrigeration), transportation (you

---

It Seemed Like a Good Idea at the Time – Desertification refers to the process that creates ever expanding deserts around the world. Allen Savory is a renowned Zimbabwean biologist and environmentalist who has led the fight to prevent desertification since the 1950s when he developed the theory that desertification was caused by overgrazing, and that the culling of grazing animals was the only way to stop it. His research was accepted and validated by scientists around the world and led to the intentional slaughter of 40,000 elephants (in the name of science) in Africa in the 1970s. Oops! It didn't seem to work as they had hoped and might not have been the best move. Though some scientists still subscribe to his early ideas, Savory calls his decision "the saddest and greatest blunder of my life," and in the mid-1980s developed a holistic land management plan to reintroduce grazing herds in an effort to prevent desertification. Sometimes we're just not as smart as we think.

can only get as far as the gas in your tank will take you), and communication (cell towers need power)? It's worth spending a couple minutes of your time at **fema.gov** to get an idea of things to consider should a real emergency happen. They even publish an Emergency Financial Aid Kit that's worth a look. Beer pong is good, but being prepared is better.

Friends

If you spend a lot of time with horse thieves, sooner or later you're going to steal a nag and get into trouble. Likewise, if all your friends are spendthrifts, you're probably going to blow your cash and be living paycheck to paycheck. Who you hang with is important. If you want to be successful and have a positive outlook on life, spend time around successful and positive people. If you don't know any successful people, then read about them and make

---

Blind Faith – During the Cold War, when NATO helicopters flew along the borders of the Warsaw Pact countries, those sneaky Russians would engage in a trick called meaconing. That's the interception and rebroadcasting of navigational signals to get the pilots to stray across the border, where they would be shot down and captured. So pilots learned not to blindly follow the needle in the cockpit without checking their position visually with known points on the ground.

Meaconing isn't a problem here at home but sometimes we can rely too much on technology. If your leaving Los Angeles to have a weekend of fun in Las Vegas and pass a signpost that says "Welcome to Arizona," it should be a hint that something is amiss. Later, when your GPS says you have 11 hours and 800 miles left in your trip, hopefully you'll realize that your headed for Las Vegas, New Mexico instead of Las Vegas, Nevada.

It's not that you shouldn't be using GPS, it's a wonderful piece of technology and probably correct 99% of the time, but you need to have a general idea of what direction you should be headed to reach your destination. Just because the GPS says turn here, doesn't always mean it's a good idea. For example: (continued on next page)

them be your role models. I've tried to highlight a few in the sidebars of this book, but you need to find your own. When you do, you'll discover that most successful people are avid readers. They would rather be educated than entertained and rarely pass up an opportunity to learn. While at Harvard, Bill Gates sat in on classes that he hadn't signed up for, just to learn something new. Surround yourself with winners, literally or figuratively.

Learn to Listen

During conversations most people spend half the time talking and half thinking about what they're going to say when it's their turn to talk again. They spend very little time actually listening. Listening, like oratory and even conversation, is becoming a lost art. We've become very impatient in a world of sound bites and tweets.

The most used word in conversation is "I," because everyone likes to talk about themselves. If you learn to become a good listener, everyone will think you are just a wonderful person. You might even make some new and interesting friends. So next time you're in a room full

> Several British workers decided to do some Christmas shopping in Lille, France but ended up in Lille, Belgium instead. (Bah Humbug!)
>
> Some Japanese tourists in Australia drove into the Pacific Ocean. (The GPS actually sent them into the mudflats and the tide came in.)
>
> Two women in Washington state drove their rented Mercedes into a lake based on bad GPS instructions. (Hertz was probably upset. Hope they had insurance.)
>
> A British woman drove her Mercedes into the River Sence. (She needed more "sense.")
>
> A limo driver in Salzburg, Austria drove his Mercedes, and his boss, down a steep flight of steps in the middle of town. (What is it about Mercedes?)
>
> Twenty-five foreign tourists were caravanning from Bryce Canyon, Utah to Grand Canyon, Arizona and became lost in the wilderness. The lead vehicle screeched to a halt just before the GPS was about to send them over a cliff. A search and rescue team got them out safely the next morning. (Welcome to America!)
>
> And my personal favorite. A truck driver left Ankara, Turkey for Gibraltar, Spain and ended up in Gibraltar Point, England, missing his destination by 1,600 miles. You'd think crossing the English Channel would have given him a clue.

of strangers ask yourself, "Am I listening to understand? Or am I just listening to respond?"

Homework

That's about all I've got to pass on about living, so if you've gotten this far I guess it's time for graduation, and that means a commencement speech and a gift. For the gift you'll have to go to the library and check out **Oh, the Places You'll Go** by Dr. Seuss and read it. As for the speech, I don't have any prepared remarks and since most commencement speeches are dreadfully boring, I'll spare you the pain of me attempting to say something profound. However there have been some great speeches to graduates over the years that are worth listening to, so grab a beverage, jump into the intergalactic web and look up the following commencement addresses:

Persistence – In his bestselling book **Things That Matter**, Pulitzer Prize winning journalist Charles Krauthammer wrote about 1999 Rookie Pitcher of the Year and St Louis Cardinal star Rick Ankiel and his historic meltdown in 2000 post-season play, when strangely he was unable to get the ball over the plate. Ankiel came back in 2001, walked 25 batters in 24 innings and was demoted to the minors. Not to be deterred, he honed his fielding and hitting skills and returned to the big leagues six years later as an outfielder, hitting a three run homer in his first game back.

But the real inspiration in Krauthammer's book is not the persistence of a baseball player, but of the author himself. An honors graduate at McGill University in Montreal, Krauthammer was offered a Commonwealth Scholarship in politics at Oxford and was also accepted to Harvard Medical school. He went to Oxford and studied for a year but then decided to pursue medicine. Near the end of his first year at Harvard, Krauthammer dove into a swimming pool, broke his neck and was hospitalized for more than a year. Not to be deterred, he had a Plexiglas frame made to hold his books above his head as he laid in bed and hired someone to turn the pages. Though wheelchair bound, Krauthammer graduated with his class and went on to become chief resident in psychiatry at Mass General.

In 1978 he moved to Washington, DC to direct some psychiatric research and began contributing articles to *The New Republic* magazine and eventually became a speechwriter for Vice President Walter Mondale. By 1981 Krauthammer was editor of *The New Republic* and also writing for *Time* and *The Washington Post* where he won a Pulitzer Prize for commentary. Today Dr. Charles Krauthammer is considered one of the most influential political commentators in America.

2005 Steve Jobs at Stanford;
2005 David Foster Wallace at Kenyon College;
2008 J K Rowling at Harvard;
2014 Admiral William McRaven at University of Texas.

Congratulations graduate! You did it!

The Bottom Line

Sometimes life demands we make simple choices, where you have to choose which path to take. You can't take them both. Think in terms of *The Matrix*. Early on Morpheus presents Neo with a choice - take the red pill and learn the painful truth about the real world or take the blue pill and remain blissfully ignorant in the status quo. Take the real life red pill and go conquer the world!

With that in mind, let's recap what was covered in this chapter.
- Money can't buy happiness but a certain amount is needed to keep misery at bay.
- Resume' virtues are good but eulogy virtues are more important.
- Don't search for the meaning of life, but seek meaning in life.
- Help the needy but not the greedy.
- Get your hands dirty and volunteer.
- Study leadership, and always remember that "the troops eat first".
- Don't judge a book by its cover.
- Health is important. Eat right, move and learn to chill.
- Give your brain a break and unplug now and then.
- Be prepared. The cyber-crooks are smarter than we are.
- Read, listen, think for yourself, and find your passion.

Epilogue

"By the time a man realizes that maybe his father was right,
he usually has a son who thinks he's wrong."
Charles Wadsworth
Bishop of St. Andrews 1852

Giving your child a skill is better than giving him a thousand pieces of gold.
Chinese proverb

"A man that views the world the same at fifty as he did at twenty
has wasted thirty years."
Muhammed Ali
Boxer

"Doing what you don't like is work. Doing what you like is play.
I have never worked a day in my life."
Leila Denmark, MD

"He who has done his best for his time has lived for all time."
Friedrich Shiller
Philospher

"Your future awaits you, so take up you responsibilities and embrace your opportunities
with enthusiasm and pride... There are no limits on how high each of you can climb."
Ronald Reagan

"What you leave behind is not what is engraved on stone monuments,
but what is woven into the lives of others."
Pericles

"Without question, the greatest invention in the history of mankind is beer.
Oh, I grant you that the wheel was also a fine invention,
but the wheel does not go nearly as well with pizza."
Dave Barry
Humorist and writer

The Intergalactic Web

It may seem that I've been dissing technology throughout the book, but please don't think I'm an angry Luddite or something. No doubt the web is the greatest thing since Dr. Alexander Nowell first bottled beer in 1570, but even the web can have its dark side. For example, after declining for many years, traffic deaths are on the rise, due in great part to distracted driving. No, the web isn't causing more accidents, just providing the distraction for idiot drivers. Self-driving cars will eventually solve that, but for now it's a killer.

The bigger problem today is that the changes the web is bringing are happening faster than the world can adjust to them or even realize what is happening. I'm not referring to using the technology, it's intuitive for you natives, but the way a tsunami of information and data is compromising our ability to think for ourselves. While this 24-7 inter-connectivity can provide us with instant news and information, it's also a platform for pundits, hate mongers, fear peddlers, and other talking heads to bombard us with their opinions and try to influence how we perceive the world. We're getting instant soundbites that distort reality and then we do things and make decisions based on incomplete knowledge of events, and facts that we assume are true. It becomes difficult to see the whole forest and not just listen to the those babbling about a couple of trees.

On a recent visit to Atlanta former New York City mayor Michael Bloomberg discussed the effects of the web on the delivery of information. He contends that since the beginning

of time, whether it was the spoken word, the written word, the printed word, radio or television, news has generally come from a verifiable source above, and flowed down to the masses. The web has turned this upside-down. Now, everyone with a smart phone is a source of unverifiable information that flows to the world instantaneously.

Bloomberg says the human brain can only absorb so

much information and we are now being inundated with bits and pieces of garbage. The media, which was once a source of legitimate news has become a purveyor of soundbites in search of advertising dollars rather than a provider of truth. When it comes to the hearts and minds of the people, this is a dangerous situation. Edgar Allen Poe wrote in 1845: "Believe nothing you hear, and only one half that you see." I think that's sage advice today. And columnist George Will says what's happening in our country today is akin to what Ferdinand VII of Spain advocated when he regained the throne in 1813 and vowed to stop "the disastrous mania of thinking."

Peanuts creator Charles Schultz said he never talked about politics, religion or The Great Pumpkin. When it comes to the first two, look before you leap. Just because someone on the idiot tube or the web says something, doesn't necessarily make it true, or mean you should swallow it hook, line and sinker. (Why would young Americans go to the sandbox and blow themselves up?) Do your own research, keep an open mind, and think for yourself. As for the Great Pumpkin, I believe Linus van Pelt never figured out that, unlike Santa, the Great Pumpkin comes to only one pumpkin patch each year and poor Linus just

---

The Maine – The media should report the news. Instead they skew it to increase readership/viewership or to sway public opinion. This is not new. Unfortunately, today questionable information can reach millions in minutes.

In January 1898 the USS Maine arrived in Havana Harbor to look after U.S. interests as Cuba was engaged in a war of independence against Spain. Three weeks later the Maine exploded, killing 258 Americans. Around the same time the *New York Journal* owned by William Randolph Hearst and the *New York World* owned by Joseph Pulitzer were locked in a fierce battle for readership. Both papers latched on to the story of the Maine, and in what became known as "yellow journalism" tried to out-sensationalize and out-exaggerate each other. They both blamed Spain and began calling for revenge. "Remember the Maine! To hell with Spain!" became the rallying cry of the day.

By April, most of the country was so worked up that Congress declared war. Assistant Secretary of the Navy Theodore Roosevelt resigned from government service to form the Rough Riders with his friend, Army doctor Leonard Wood, who was President McKinley's personal physician. After their famous charge up San Juan Hill, TR rode his horse all the way to the White House. Dr. Wood, who's remarkable career included a Medal of Honor and serving as the first football coach at Georgia Tech, became Military Governor of Cuba.

The cause of the explosion was never fully determined. Most likely a boiler exploded aboard the ship.

keeps picking the wrong one. But I certainly do admire him for his unshakable belief and maintaining his vigilance.

Would You Like Fries With That?

You're in the drive-thru lane at the Burger-Doodle House; you pull up to the menu board and the voice-in-the-box asks for your order. So you order a bacon wrapped bacon sandwich with cheese and extra jalapenos, and the voice-in-the-box asks if you'd like fries with that, then tells you to pull around to the window. There you come face to face with the person who took your order. The question is: Does that person have to be in that building? Couldn't the job be done from down the street or across town? In a wired world, couldn't Burger-Doodle House have a single call center with a herd of operators taking orders for hundreds of restaurants? After all, that person is just entering the order into a computer for the cooks in the kitchen.

In **The World is Flat**, Pulitzer Prize-winning author Thomas Friedman tells how the interconnected world is changing the way we work. Boeing runs two shifts of Russian engineers out of Moscow for about one third the cost per design hour of their counterparts in Seattle, and more than a million U.S. personal tax returns are completed in India each year for large American accounting firms. The possibilities are endless. Friedman says the thing that just might save us is our imagination. Americans, due in large part to our culture, are creative and resourceful, and that's a big advantage in a fast-moving, ever-changing technological world. I hope he's right.

I learned first-hand about this changing workplace one night several years ago when James suffered a head injury while playing football. At the ER they did a CAT scan to check that his brain was still all in one piece, and then we had to wait for a radiologist to read the scan. It was taking quite a while so I finally asked if the radiologist had arrived yet, and was told that the scan was digital and the radiologist was actually in an office 15 miles away. That radiologist could just as easily have been in India. The takeaway here is that for many jobs you don't have to be physically "in the office" and can work from home, even if it's in another country.

In some fields the workplace is evolving into what's referred to as a Results Only Work Environment (ROWE), where employees are paid for results and not for the number of hours worked, which can lead to improved worker satisfaction and productivity. It doesn't matter if you work from Kathmandu or Timbuktu, as long as you get the job done. The one thing that will be required to survive and thrive in a ROWE world is discipline, because now you aren't just in competition with 80 million other American Millennials, you're potentially competing with  hundreds of millions of Millennials around the world. For a generation that grew up with a pat on the back, a slice of pizza and a "participation trophy" for every endeavor no matter the effort, this new world may come as a challenge. No one will be there to hold your hand and provide a "safe space" to shield you from reality, but I have faith that you can do it.

For some of you this was a book about a subject in which you had little interest, yet you finished it. That's discipline. Now that you're done I hope you realize nearly everything you read about in these pages required discipline. Times change and so will you, but no matter how you change, discipline is the one constant if you are to reach your full potential in life.

It takes discipline to pay yourself first and save while living in a consumer society.
It takes discipline to keep your fingers out of the emergency fund, except in an emergency.
It takes discipline to create a budget and stick with it.
It takes discipline to continue investing when the market is falling.
It takes discipline to live like a hermit to get out of debt when your friends are living large.
It takes discipline to choose an affordable education and graduate in four years.
It takes discipline not to borrow for lifestyle.
It takes discipline to develop delayed gratification.
It takes discipline to follow your passion, even if it doesn't bring you riches.
It takes discipline to get off your butt and move.
It takes discipline to place your eulogy virtues above your resume virtues.
It takes discipline to eat right in a junk food world.
It takes discipline to unplug from the wired world every now and then.
It takes discipline to not be judgmental and be nice to a turd-head.
It takes discipline to not touch that cellphone while driving.
It takes discipline to think for yourself.
It takes discipline to drink responsibly.

Thank You

I appreciate you buying the book and hope you gained something from it. It was meant to educate and entertain. If all you remember is that Beer Pong was invented at Dartmouth or that the Romans used pee for mouthwash, then I failed at the former and succeeded at the latter. With every point I tried to get across, never was I blowing smoke, and always tried to tell it as I saw it. If you enjoyed it, will you take a moment to leave a review where you bought the book?

The ball really is in your court when it comes to your future, but with a little knowledge

> **Blowing Smoke –** When tobacco first arrived from the New World, European doctors were quick to recognize its medicinal qualities and before long were using it to treat colds and drowsiness. Later they learned that the North American natives performed tobacco smoke enemas, so the British docs adopted the practice and were soon pumping smoke in patients' butts. It became a mainstream treatment for gut pain, headaches, hernias, cholera, typhoid, cancer and even to revive people dead from drowning. In 1774 doctors William Hawes and Thomas Cogan founded The Institution For Affording Immediate Relief to Persons Apparently Dead From Drowning (whew!) which was later shortened to The Royal Humane Society. They strategically placed resuscitation kits along the Thames and other waterways - much like we have AEDs in airports and malls. When needed, a tube attached to a bellows was inserted into a victim's rectum and tobacco smoke was pumped in. If that didn't work they would switch ends and pump smoke into the lungs (hope they changed tubes) to warm the heart and dry out the victim's insides. Should that fail, bloodletting was the last option.
>
> By 1811 it was decided that nicotine was toxic and smoke enemas fell out of favor, but Danish farmers continued to use them for many years on horses in need of a laxative.
>
> Makes you wonder what state-of-the-art, mainstream treatments we're using today, that in a century or so, they'll look back on and say: "OMG! How could they have done that?"

and a level head I know you'll be successful. We old farts are counting on you. Then again, we have no other choice.

I'd like to leave you with one final thought. Beginning in 2025, less than a decade from now, thousands of Boomers will be turning 80 every single day. Dementia is probably going to be a huge problem. So if someday in the future, you find me wandering aimlessly about in Lala Land with a note pinned to my shirt, stop me and read the note. It will say: "Buy this man a beer." Thanks.

For My Sons

Boys,

As all parents know or will learn, when it comes to raising children, the days are long and the years are short. I first conceived the idea of writing this book for y'all in 2004, but didn't get past the scribbled-notes-on-scraps-of-paper stage until the beginning of 2011. It was to be your Christmas gift that year, but after several months of diligent effort, life got in the way and it collected dust until it became my New Year's resolution for 2015. Determined to finish, I spent about every free hour I could working on it, but discovered it took a lot longer to research and write than I anticipated. Then I learned that the writing part is only the beginning. Publishing is a whole nother ballgame. So now 2016 is drawing to a close and y'all are grown and out of the nest, but as they say, better late than never.

Hindsight can sometimes be a wonderful thing, maybe not so much as a "Monday morning quarterback" for your favorite team, but to look back at some of the decisions one has made in life. We all should do it more often. When I looked back and saw some of the stupid and asinine decisions I've made over the years I knew I had to make an effort to help you guys avoid doing the same things. This book is that effort. I hope you enjoy it.

I want you to know that I'm very proud of each of you and offer the following thoughts:

Spend more time thinking about ideas and less time talking about people.
May you find happiness and someone to share it with.
Try to see the forest and not just the trees.
Stop to smell the roses along life's way.
Strive to reach your potential.
Take care of your mother.
Go beyond your limits.
Unplug now and then.
Never stop learning.
Eat your veggies.
Don't complain.
Laugh often.
Love,
Dad

Stardust -- I have to throw in one last sidebar for my grandchildren, Christian, Jack and Dylan, who are all big fans of Neil deGrasse Tyson and his amazing descriptions of the universe. When the Big Bang happened (I was just a kid) very light hydrogen and helium atoms were formed, but as stars were created, heavier elements were made. After a big star gets old it collapses into a dense ball and dies in an explosion called a supernovae that scatters its atoms throughout the galaxy, which are then used to form new stars, planets, moons, water, monkeys, worms, dogs, cats, people and other stuff. So all the carbon, oxygen, nitrogen, calcium and other atoms that make up out bodies come from the dust of exploding stars long, long ago. Scientists estimate there are about 7,000,000,000,000,000,000,000,000,000 (that's 27 zeros) atoms in a human body, and when measured by mass, we are 93% stardust. Next time you step on a scale, think about that.

About the Author

Years ago Barry Pencek decided that he would someday write a book for his four sons, to pass along to them some common sense and practical advice on finance, among other things. In 2006, after a career flying with the Marine Corps and several airlines, he began volunteering at consumer advocate Clark Howard's Consumer Action Center, answering phone calls from across the country. It was then that he realized that it wasn't just his sons in need of such advice, but the entire "younger generation," so his family project morphed into *The Millennial's Guide to Wealth*.

Barry resides in suburban Atlanta, GA with the love of his life Mary, and spends most of his time reading, writing, tinkering and drinking the occasional beer.

Half of any money earned from the sale of this book will be split between the following two charities:

The Marine Corps Scholarship Foundation (MCSF)
Honoring Marines by Educating Their Children has been the mission of the MCSF since 1962. Over the last 54 years the foundation has provided more than 35,000 need-based scholarships to the children of Marines and Navy Corpsmen that served with them. The best part of it is that 50% of the recipients are the first in their families to go to college, 45% are STEM and health sciences majors, and they have an 86% graduation rate. More information can be found at **mcsf.org**.

The International Essential Tremor Foundation (IETF)
Eight times more common than Parkinson's disease, Essential Tremor (ET) is a neurological condition that causes trembling of the hands, head, and voice and can become disabling. Yet it's the condition that no one has ever heard of. Because of stereotypes and lack of awareness, many ET suffers never seek treatment. The IETF was founded in 1988 as a non-profit membership organization and funds research to find the cause of ET and provide educational materials, tools, and support for health-care providers and those affected by ET. You can learn more at **essentialtremor.org**.

Photo Credits

Unless otherwise indicated, the rights to use photos, charts and other illustrations in this publication were purchased from one of the sources listed below unless availlable in the public domain or as a function of the Fair Use doctrine.

Barry Pencek – pages xii, 146,

123rf.com – pages xiii, xv, 4, 8, 10, 13, 14, 16, 18, 20, 36, 40, 46, 47, 49, 55, 59, 66, 68, 69, 75, 84, 88, 90, 93, 94, 95, 98, 99, 100, 103, 104, 105, 106, 110, 111, 114, 115, 118, 119, 120, 125, 127, 133, 136, 138, 139, 144, 146, 147, 148, 150, 153, 155, 157, 158, 159, 160, 161, 162, 166, 169, 171, 172

Public domain – pages 3, 5, 6, 12, 25, 32, 42, 52, 89, 96, 121, 173

Dollarphotoclub.com – pages 28, 56, 58, 80, 101, 151

Josh Langston – page 78

Random House – page 142

www.ingramcontent.com/pod-product-compliance
Lightning Source LLC
Chambersburg PA
CBHW081146180526
45170CB00006B/1946